Imagine Unity: Bridging Divides

Tony Churchill

Published by Tony Churchill, 2024.

Imagine Unity

Bridging Divides

by Tony Churchill

IMAGINE UNITY: BRIDGING DIVIDES

First edition. April 22, 2024.

Copyright © 2024 Tony Churchill.

ISBN: 979-8224316052

Written by Tony Churchill.

Table of Contents

Epigraph

"No change for the better has ever come without someone first standing to say it was needed. I, for one, shall stand."

~ ~ Tony L. Churchill

Foreword

Before anyone gets their wires crossed or jumps to conclusions, let's clarify a critical point about John Lennon's song "Imagine," which Tony Churchill explores in this compelling new book. In undertaking this analysis, Mr. Churchill demonstrates considerable audacity by presenting such idealistic views amidst our present chaotic, degenerative and unsustainable political environment.

It is essential to recognize that while some have hastily labeled "Imagine" as communist, this interpretation does not capture the song's essence. Lennon's vision, beautifully articulated through his lyrics, envisions a utopia marked by peace, unity, and global harmony; a vision that transcends the boundaries of any specific political doctrine, especially those as stringent as communism.

Communism, as an ideology, proposes a classless society where all property and resources are collectively owned, and personal property is abolished. This system often necessitates authoritarian governance, where dissent is suppressed, and freedoms are curtailed. Historically, communism has been implemented through centralized, authoritarian regimes that are antithetical to the free-spirited harmony Lennon imagined.

On the other hand, socialism, though sometimes conflated with communism, generally supports social ownership of production means alongside the right to personal property. It aims to redistribute wealth through progressive policies within a democratic framework, ensuring personal freedoms are maintained.

John Lennon's "Imagine" does not advocate for these or any political systems explicitly. Instead, it promotes a dreamlike vision of global togetherness devoid of materialism, nationalism, and religious barriers. This song is a poetic call for universal peace and brotherhood, clearly opposing any form of authoritarian governance.

As a professor commenting on this ambitious work, I see Mr. Churchill's exploration of "Imagine" as not merely an academic exercise but as a crucial reflection on the enduring power of hope and the vast potential for human kindness in times of division. This book challenges us to consider Lennon's message of unity and peace as not only conceivable but essential.

This book invites readers to engage deeply with Lennon's timeless vision. Mr. Churchill's work encourages us to reflect on how we can embody these ideals in our own lives and communities, promoting a world bound not by geopolitical lines or dogmatic views but by mutual respect and love.

Let us embark on this journey with open hearts and minds, inspired by Tony Churchill's insightful interpretations and the enduring legacy of John Lennon's dream.

Welcome to a thought-provoking exploration of what it might mean to truly live as one.

~ ~ Professor Cyril Masterson, Arcadian Institute of Cultural Studies

Prologue

"You may think I'm a dreamer, but I'm not the only one."

As I sit down to write this, I can't help but think about the dreamers. You know, those of us who think of things that sound improbable, that look beyond what is and see what could be. You might fancy dismissing such trains of thought as mere fancy, illusions that dissipate with the soft light of dawn. The fact is that I would not be alone . No, dreaming is a human reality. It is what pushes us, inspires us and through its flame, we innovate. Everything, every step that has been a watershed moment in any sense, began as a dream. It is a vision of a better future, in which people exist in a better world; one with muted bullies, healed divides and absent fear. And that isn't a fantasy either; it's as close to the future as we will ever get. So if dreaming is a part of our human nature, then so is dreaming a big dream. So let us dream. And let's dream so furiously and with such passion for making a new reality that reality will have no choice but to follow.

I write this not just as an opening to a set of ideals laid down on paper, but as an invitation; a call to enter into a movement that transcends these pages, borders and our lifetimes. It's a call to all who have ever looked out at the world and seen potential, the question of "what if?" beckoning to them. This book is for all who have had the daring to think that the future can be made into what we what it to be now, that this radical imagining can be applied to radical doing. In the pages to come, we will walk together over the churned earth of a world remade. We will examine the twin pillars of a shared earth, echoing not from our pockets but the community trust and the halcyon era of peace that will take hold of our hearts, that will oust our wars. I hope that every word will resonate, every lesson inspire, perhaps even to call into being our deeds. But also, I want to reassure than you are not alone in dreaming this dream. Across the globe, countless others imagine this world. We are only humble weavers in a veiled scarf of dreamer sewing the cloth of a different tomorrow. These dreams are not simple wishes and whims; they are plans, sketches for building something big. This book should serve as a reminder that the act of dreaming is in itself a form of planning. Only when we perceive alternative realities can we begin to imagine the reality. Only when we see optimism we realize change is it possible.

So as you turn these pages, let your imagination soar. In your wildest dreams, imagine a world in which love conquers fear, in which togetherness overcomes disunity, in which the human spirit is honored in every shape and form. And always remember: every person who dreams with us brings us one step closer to making that dream come true. Let's dream big and work hard. Dream together, help shape the future. It's within our power to do so! This is more than just a book. It's a lighthouse. It's a map to a better future. Join me. Join us. And let's bring these dreams to life!

Part 1: No Heaven or Hell

Here, we get to engage in a deep and thought-provoking exploration of the possibility of society's nature if we were to abandon the constructs of heaven and hell. What would the world look like if we were not to be encouraged and deterred by promises of rewards and threats of perdition for eternity? What if we didn't act in ethical ways for some spiritual reward that happens after we die but instead did this because what is right here and now? This is a fascinating subject to explore: what would society be like if we as humans did our best to do our duties here on earth for their own sake. I believe that the change would be monumental: that our general interaction and judgement of one another as members of the human would change. This reimagined world will be about creating a need to fulfill the human experience and that might create a society which is more compassionate and pragmatic in nature. This is about creating a society that makes decisions based on today, rather than centuries to come. It might dissolve our many fears and prejudices and be more companionate, aspiring to define what a good life means. In this society, our morality changes to focus on today rather than abstract or future events, driving us to act kindly today, but not punish bad behavior because we can gain ours here and now.

Furthermore, this part of the book insists on asking readers what life would be without the binary judgment that good deserves heaven and bad deserve hell. can we forgive and can we grow in the same community? I shall also elaborate more on how this philosophy would affect leadership and government and how, without the prop of divine right and absolute good and evil, those in power would have no alternative but to adopt their policies and actions focused on real-world consequences and ethical practicality. Moreover, the emphasis was not just theoretical; it was an urging to re-evaluate and redevelop our values, our laws, our educational institutions and even the behavior of our people on a daily basis. It was an explanation in the concept renaissance of how to contemplate one's own virtuousness, vice and the meaning of life. I urge you to consider, investigate and modify and, in doing so, not just your own life but also the course of all humanity: not to reconsider the meaning of authentic over non-human or sensual over mystical living. As long as realistic stories, thought-provoking analysis and real-life lessons are shared, this section of the book still does its utmost to justify how much our comprehension of the life following death has seeped through and affects our earthly behaviors.

Chapter 1: Awakening to Reality

The more I thought about it, the more it felt like waking up from a deep, long sleep. It was the growing feeling of realization that perhaps we never needed to feel chained by this knowledge in the first place. What if the very concept of afterlife had no real reason to haunt us like some sort of cosmic jailer, inspiring fear and forcing us to try and pass all kinds of checkpoints for a chance to enter some kind of realm meticulously described by a multitude of religions? It all seemed so arbitrary. What gave these beliefs the right to define how we treat each other in this life? What gave them the right to define our laws, our politics, our very joy of living? Taking off this shroud of shackles made me wonder what kind of a world we would have if we have all agreed we only live for here and for now. What if we have all agreed to entirely ignore the fantastic that may or may not exist and make the best of what we definitely have – a physical world that we can all touch and experience? The idea was both empowering and horrifying. How would our goals change if we're no longer striving to get somewhere "good"? What if we have agreed to make our world the best place to live here and now? Naturally, I began discussing this idea with people. At first, it was just casual talks. Naturally, many were reluctant to take the conversation seriously. The idea of discarding the heaven-and-hell narrative as the guiding principle of our societal structure seemed abhorrent to most, maybe even heretical. However, as we talked, I began seeing genuine curiosity in their eyes. It was as though they have suddenly seen a door open before them, revealing a realm of possibilities where the fundamentals of motivation and purpose were wide open for reshaping.

Honestly, I found the world hereafter concept so removed from reality that it slowly percolated to all aspects of life. It led me to envision a society where the only measure of an action or decision was the actual terrestrial outcomes rather than some intuitive metaphysical consequences. Perhaps education was no longer aimed at enforcing fear and revulsion towards divine punishment; perhaps the only virtues it rewarded were they of compassion and responsibility and innovation. Maybe the laws no more attempt at compelling religious overtones but ones demanding fairness and defending the permission to live the truthful life so far as its lie does not cross that of others. And what struck the most was nothing but the prospect that this life and all the discord and separation arose from the difference in beliefs on who we would be after our demise. What would exist with a common grounding in nonexistence? What would daily life and the essence of existence appear without the comforting assuredness in a second scope? And something moreover altered everything. From politics, to business, to life attitude, -alia became absorbed with the concept of 'reality-first.' It transformed the way I considered allocation of resources, social systems, rightfulness. If this is the sole chance we get and all we do, how severely and promptly would we fix the inequality, poverty and warmth?

But truly waking up means ditching not just our old beliefs. This time, we also take responsibility for our legacy right here and now, in the flesh and blood world that our grandchildren will inherit. We decide for real this time to care about the real, to prioritize it above the imagined, the promised. And you know what? Once you do that; if you do that; there is no going back. For the first time, truly awake, every moment adds up. You add them up to make something truly worthwhile. Every decision has weight, has responsibility. You realize only through your account can you see the world for what it is. And it's about time.

Chapter 2: The Disillusionment of Dogma

I grew up with a big and dark idea of what lay in store after this life. Heaven, hell; the idea was so much more than just stories or theories. Instead, they were the ultimate destinations: How well you played by the rules determined how much time you would spend at either end. But as I grew up and hopefully a little wiser, the idea didn't sit so easily with me. It was like pulling a strand from a sweater. The threads quickly unraveled the more I began to question everything I had ever accepted. The idea of eternal reward or eternal punishment seemed less like guidance or inspiration and more like coercion and control. The more I thought about it, the more I thought about how heavily theological overhead costs influenced not just our moral behavior, but our societies' behavior, our governments' behavior and our personal behavior. I remember sitting in a cafe one rainy afternoon, watching people walk by and I thought about how different everything would look if we didn't have this version of one after. What if we, instead, put all that energy into this life? I wondered about what the world would look like if we put everything we had into making life better for everyone in the world, rather than preparing for a life that none of us could be sure even existed.

So, the connection between morality and ethics and religious belief was clearly as ridiculous as it sounded. Why would one need the heaven promise to do good? Why can't I do good just because it makes the world slightly kinder? These kinds of questions led me to exploring secular humanism, which, I should say, really hit the spot. I mean, it is based on trying to accomplish and help others, except not according to anything someone told me to do. Rather, it is anything everyone agrees does make people generally happier and better together. This was liberating for sure, but it also meant a test. Saying goodbye to the promised afterlife justice world was work, I admit. It was like losing a gigantic safety net, which is always there, attempting to convince you that the world is ultimately just after all. But it also felt like opening my eyes, allowing me to better see real-life things that could be done here and now. It was not about nihilism or getting myself another version of the worst of my spirituality in those times; it rather made me ground those spiritual visions in real-world issues and contacts.

My engaging with other people who agreed or disagreed with these beliefs started to matter more profoundly. It was no longer about saving someone's soul but more rather how I could do something that could help us or how that one's venture suiting their needs was also what mine should support. It was no longer turning to be philosophy but my aspiration. I wanted to create a society where people could live together and individually. I mean, not in the old idea of sin meet purgatory. Instead, I mean coming up with a live definition of good for everyone, making it clearer and clearer due to its practice.

Infections with this new perspective also transformed my actions and interactions. It was not about removing all my spiritual views, but instead rewinding them in such a way that they converged on the earthbound desires. How can we make the world more equitable, nicer and compassionate? How do we construct a society where people are valued only for their constructive actions and not on their proximity to traditional beliefs? These are the questions that drive us and serve as the foundation for everything I do – from how I vote for to whom I donate, to those I talk with both friends and strangers. In a way, this introduction to dogma has been a reflection to what is really essential. It isn't about what would be an event to us after passing, but what we do now that we are here. It isn't about the spiritual bequest but rather the practical changes we bring through our love and the progressive changes that support everyone. And it is through the relaxation of those antiquated concepts that I develop stronger belief, because now I completely believe in humanity and the influence we can exert while we are all in it for the current.

Chapter 3: Embracing Earthly Existence

This exploration is about what it would be like to truly lean into our earthly existence. It's about living as though there isn't an after, about recognizing that what we have right now is so profoundly precious and deserving of our complete attention and reverence. I start to wonder, what if we really lived as though this was it? No future hope of an afterlife to set things straight, no otherworldly reward to look forward to. We'd be so much more present to everything; our planet, our societies and ourselves. How intense would that be? Living life without the promise of some mystical afterlife as recompense for the one we've got here; now that would completely alter the landscape. It would take away the safety net for sure. But it would chuck us into the fires of immediate, unfiltered accountability for how we treat it all. Things like legacy, impact and kindness wouldn't be thoughtful extras; they'd be non-negotiable, core parts of a resonant, meaningful existence. It's like finding out that we're all at the wheel, on this big, open road. And every choice we make, every turn we take, really matters, not merely to us but to all the other drivers. And it isn't just about undoing the afterlife; it's about celebrating the fleeting beauty of the only one thing we know for sure. The way the sun comes through the leaves in the morning, the sound of your friend laughing, the feeling of being home wherever that is, all of these apparently ordinary essentials become so sacred because they're all that we have. Instead of making them feel inconsequential, their impermanence makes them feel more tremendous somehow.

Maybe some of us are already living in such a scenario. Just the policies and the whole education system focused on our maximal utility and maximum well-being and ecological health here and now. I have feelings we would live in more sustainable depends to our own resources, I have strong feelings we would much more often live in a way that may include maximal utility for every one of us, which means being able to live, not only survive. The education system would be done for a wise and compassionate human, not just to work or innovate. And what about us? How do we act in this new world? We have to live now. We have to look at our surroundings and our insides. We have to do everything to remember about the indirect influence of every action or decision of ours. We have to redefine our standards for a good life. It's not the number of things we own, not the amount of accomplished things, it's experiencing meaningful relationships, being kind to others, bettering what we can. Living earthly living is radical action, it's a real promise to live, love and do as little harm as we can. That honesty means life for a few and trying to do everything with a smile on one's face in the meantime. Because if that's everything, these few decades or hey, maybe only moments, on Earth, then each of them is a priceless gift. And what could be more spiritual than that?

Chapter 4: Journeys Beyond Fear

The thought of what life would be like if we weren't so afraid began to take me down a new trail of thought. It's not a question of throwing out consequences or choosing to act with no respect for others. It's a matter of living unrestricted in the present, celebrating life for its sake and not for where it may lead us after we're gone. This journey started with one simple question: what if we weren't afraid? Not just of what happens after we pass on, but of everything else that comes with 'after'; like after we fail, after we choose, after we love. What if it didn't equate to eternal judgment?

Then, I started to imagine a day without that fear. When I awoke, the sun seemed a bit brighter, elevated by no sacred standards. I made decisions based on my impulses, not weighed down by the thoughts of an eternal reward. This liberated me. I was truer to myself than ever and I have never been more morally open than when I ignored the amendment. I wasn't afraid of going to hell, but instead, I was focused on attempting to create a sanctuary right here.

As I communicated this idea to others, I observed something unusual. Conversations were no longer about measuring life experiences against ethics established by an unseen force. Instead, everyone focused on learning from and living through their experiences, not preaching.

I remember one particular afternoon. I was sitting with a group of old friends and for the first time, we did not circumvent the topics that we used to tip-toe around. We discussed our beliefs or rather, the absence thereof. What else was life for, if not to prepare for an afterlife? We talked about how to make a mark on the world here and now, about being kind because kindness makes the world a better place today, not because it promises a reward tomorrow.

This new perspective shifted how I understood courage and bravery. It was no longer about grand gestures or heroic acts. It was about the silent bravery of living authentically. Each day without that ancient fear was a step toward a more genuine existence. I found new resources of courage, not because I wasn't afraid, but because I was no longer afraid of being wrong in the eyes of a judgmental god.

As I journeyed beyond fear, I understood that a life without that fear was fuller. It was about filling my day with actions that had an immediately positive impact. Volunteering, lending a helping hand, showing up; not to earn points with the Almighty, but because it's what makes human life so beautiful and connected.

The journey beyond fear isn't about discarding all caution. It's about recalibrating why we do what we do. Are we acting out of fear or love? Are we motivated by punishment or by passion? When the threat of eternal damnation is off the table, there's only the present to consider. Fear is no longer the driver; it simply serves as a reminder of what's at stake if we forget to live fully and kindly in the now. And honestly, living like this has made all the difference.

Chapter 5: Liberation from the Afterlife

The afterlife was a major deal in my community growing up. Every choice and moment was overshadowed by this enormous outcome. Heaven, hell; couldn't the stakes be any higher? However, what if we cleared that slate? What if we erased the barrier between this life and the supposed next and focused purely on the present? That's what I've been contemplating and let me tell you, it's been enlightening. It feels like I've just come up for a crisp, refreshing breath of air, free from the threat of an afterlife holding me back. It doesn't negate anyone's religious beliefs; instead, it poses the question, "What if we narrowed our focus a bit more?" We often get so caught up in what's next that we overlook the present; the here and now, the only thing we truly know we have.

I began to imagine what it would be like if everyone lived this way. Imagine a life where actions aren't driven by the fear of eternal damnation or the allure of eternal bliss. Instead, motivations stem from a desire to make the world better right now, not just for ourselves but for everyone. It's about making the most of our time on Earth because that's what we can see, touch and influence.

Talking to people who have adopted this worldview reveals a recurring theme of relief. It's as though a weight has been lifted. They're no longer burdened by the fear that every little action has eternal consequences. Instead, they're empowered to do good for the sake of goodness, to find joy in the here and now and to help others do the same.

Of course, this shift isn't without its challenges. It requires a profound change in perspective, a new ethical foundation. How do we define what's good without celestial oversight? It turns out, we look around. We consider the well-being of others. We assess the immediate impacts of our actions on our surroundings and societies and act from a place of empathy and compassion.

It might sound fantastical, but isn't it also wonderful? To think that we could catalyze such compassion and change not by looking to the skies, but by looking at each other and our world. This isn't about removing the comfort that beliefs in an afterlife provide for many; it's about exploring the potential of fully embracing life before death, the realities we can see and influence.

Living without the specter of an afterlife doesn't make life less meaningful. On the contrary, it makes every day more precious, every relationship more valuable and every action more impactful. We are liberated from fear, from hesitation, from the shadows of what might come after. This freedom allows us to take bolder steps toward improving our world, to cherish each moment and to create a legacy of positivity and progress that lives on in memories, in stories and in the tangible improvements we make to our world. Isn't that a kind of immortality worth striving for?

Chapter 6: Personal Faith in a Shared World

What does personal faith mean in a world where traditional religious structures have given way to an interconnected, shared culture of inclusion? That's a complicated question. Personal faith implies a person's private beliefs about the world, yet it is also subject to the rules of coexistence observed by society. It is a kind of delicate balance on the razor's edge. On one hand, there are certain spiritual or existential facts that you consider to be true, while on the other, there is a varied picture of beliefs in society that try to influence your thinking.

I first think about my own faith. During my development, faith was obtained by default. It is generally accepted that people adopt the religion that their parents have chosen for them. But in this thought experiment, we are talking about a world where the religion of the family is not mentored. This is a quite dynamic religion, in which beliefs change with the people with whom you communicate. Faith does not consist of you "fitted" into the box. This is a long journey looking for all those pieces of the puzzle that will help you understand what your life goal is. However, personal faith is only a small ripple in the ocean. I also think about society, in which personal faith exists like many threads of different colors in a woven picture. Indeed, in a world like this, the world would be many times prettier.

How can you keep your own beliefs when everyone is touting secularism as the new creed? How can you practice your body and soul in a way that is true to who you are, yet, at the same time, respects the fact that there are others who follow a different spiritual path or don't have a spiritual path at all? It is a matter of balance and courtesy, as everyone's voice should be heard, even if this voice elects to remain silent where their faith is concerned. As I consider this, I realize how important communication is in this new age of tolerance. It is not so much what I believe or don't, but listening to what others have to say. This dialogue is not about striking others for your side, but about learning to see the beauty of a big whole that is human experience and human understanding. What excites me the most is how much growth is possible in such an environment. There is always a new perspective, a fresh way of looking at one's surroundings. Sure, it is challenging, but it makes your faith grow, it makes your vision of the world more complete. It is like each interaction leaves a mark on you and, slowly but surely, grows into the whole picture. What is more, faith is not a way to prove that you are different from all the others; it becomes a way to connect with them. It is a bridge, not a wall. It is a way to learn to appreciate life together and order what we have learned through our shared experience without renouncing what we had possessed before that.

Ultimately, this vision of the mingling world does not cheapen the message of faith. It instead gives faith a place in the dock where it lives and expands and blends into a vibrant human artistic creation. In this reality, faith – my faith – feels more real, fully my own, struggling, unveiling and experiencing it as sincerely as good companions from all over the world.

Chapter 7: Society's New Values

Let's consider what happens when the world truly begins to value life here and now, without the hypothetical rewards of an afterlife or the threats of eternal damnation. It's quite an intriguing shift. We begin to redefine "normal" behavior, driven not by potential outcomes after death but by achievable and tangible goals in our present reality.

So, what changes? Quite a lot. People start prioritizing actions that have immediate, concrete benefits. This includes increasing charitable contributions, enhancing community projects and adopting sustainable living practices. It seems that once the incentives of heaven and the fear of hell are removed, the present moment gains newfound importance.

Ethically, it becomes a roller coaster initially. Without the conventional religious moral compass, people begin to ask, "What now guides us?" This leads to the emergence of "practical ethics," principles that are grounded and focused on improving everyone's life right now. Fairness, equity and respect become the cornerstones of this new moral framework.

Education transforms as well. Instead of teaching right and wrong based solely on traditional doctrines, schools encourage critical thinking about ethics and the real-world impacts of our choices. Students explore a diverse range of cultural and philosophical perspectives, fostering greater tolerance and understanding.

The workplace experiences a profound shift too. Companies start to genuinely implement corporate social responsibility, not as a public relations strategy but as a fundamental operational ethos. Businesses aim to benefit all stakeholders, including employees, communities and the environment, because it's now seen as the ethical norm.

The media also changes its approach, focusing more on stories that explore ethical dilemmas and their resolutions. There's a surge in coverage of acts of kindness and collaborative efforts across societies, which helps cultivate a culture where being recognized for contributing to societal well-being becomes more desirable than fame for wealth or scandals.

Even the arts reflect this change, with movies, books and music delving into the complexities of living ethically in a world devoid of spiritual absolutes.

Artists take on the role of exploring and depicting what it means to live a meaningful life based solely on present realities.

These changes aren't just ripples; they're tidal waves. As people begin living more for today than for some uncertain tomorrow, anxiety about the afterlife diminishes and engagement with current issues increases. Mental health improves as communities become stronger and individuals feel more connected and supported in their immediate environments.

This shift in values brings humanity to a pivotal moment. It's about embracing life as we know it, with all its challenges and joys and I find myself incredibly optimistic about it. As we focus on making the present as fulfilling as possible, not only do we enhance our own lives, but we also lay the foundation for future generations to thrive in a world that's more thoughtful, fair and engaged.

Chapter 8: Ethics Without Absolutes

Exploring a world where ethics are not bound by strict absolutes brings up intriguing considerations. It's fascinating to envision morality detached from stringent, prescriptive codes or any particular belief system. When ethics are liberated from fixed rules, they pivot more towards empathy, context and the common good, rather than strictly adhered-to regulations.

This fundamental shift transforms our societal interactions. Decision-making becomes less about checking off a list of 'dos and don'ts' and more about deeply considering the impact of our actions on others. It emphasizes tuning into the complexities of real-world situations and responding with compassion and fairness.

Without absolute ethics, we engage in what can be described as situational ethics, where moral reasoning is dynamic and contextual. This isn't about abandoning moral considerations but adapting our ethical compass to a more nuanced appreciation of human needs and circumstances. We find ourselves in a continuous dialogue with the world, where our actions are considered not just for their immediate effects but also for their wider implications.

Principles like equity, respect and sustainability guide our actions instead of fear of divine judgment or societal retribution. This approach encourages us to be more reflective and conscientious about our interactions and the choices we make.

Consider everyday decisions, like whether to speak up when something doesn't feel right. It's no longer just about the potential personal consequences; retribution or praise; but about evaluating the broader impact of one's actions. Questions like "What does the most good here?" or "How can I help make this situation better for everyone involved?" become central to our decision-making process.

Transitioning to this kind of ethical thinking doesn't guarantee that we'll always make the right decisions. Human error is inevitable, but the focus shifts towards learning from these mistakes to enhance our understanding of what it means to live ethically in a way that respects and uplifts all of humanity.

This paradigm also emphasizes the critical role of education. From a young age, there would be a need to teach not only critical thinking but also empathy, ethical reasoning and conflict resolution. Imagine schools that view ethics not as a set of rigid rules but as a fluid, ongoing project that students continuously engage with.

Leadership too must evolve in this landscape. Leaders need to be adaptive, insightful and transparent as they navigate these complex moral terrains without clear-cut answers, making decisions that are best for their communities.

Embracing ethics without absolutes isn't about eliminating moral standards; instead, it enriches them. It fosters a more flexible, responsive approach to living that adapts to the constant changes in our global society. This shift is both thrilling and daunting but holds the promise of creating a more thoughtful, inclusive and compassionate world.

Chapter 9: Celebrating the Secular

Embarking on a journey inspired by John Lennon's vision in "Imagine," we explore the profound notion of embracing a secular life where society cherishes the present, not just the potential of an afterlife. This idea paints a landscape rich with pragmatism and a collective celebration of our current existence.

Imagine a world where our daily actions aren't dictated by religious doctrines but driven by a universal respect for human dignity and equality. In this world, holidays wouldn't commemorate religious figures or events but would celebrate human achievements across science, heroism and the arts. It's about recognizing human progress and the collective journey of our species.

The beauty of this secular celebration isn't about diminishing joy or reverence in our lives; rather, it aims to enrich our calendar with festivities that bring us together rather than divide. We could establish days dedicated to the celebration of human culture, advancements in science and technology, and even simple joys of human connection.

Education would also transform, with schools teaching moral philosophy and ethics outside of a religious framework. The curriculum would be laden with stories of historical and contemporary figures who have shaped the world through their resilience and ingenuity, not divine inspiration.

In the public sphere, this shift would mean that political debates and policies are grounded in immediate needs; like poverty, education, healthcare and environmental sustainability; addressed through reason and evidence rather than religious belief. Guiding principles would include empathy, fairness and a profound responsibility for the well-being of every community member.

This secular approach also introduces a new kind of freedom; the liberty to follow one's spiritual path without external pressure or prejudice. Whether one finds meaning in religion, nature, science or humanitarian efforts, all choices are respected equally.

Adopting secularism in public life doesn't banish religion but prevents it from dictating public affairs. Instead, we unite under universally agreeable values like kindness, justice and innovation. This reimagining promises a refreshing change; a society that celebrates our shared human journey and builds an educational system that equips individuals to live ethically and joyfully in a diverse world.

It's a bold vision but one that could lead to a more unified and peaceful existence, where the focus is on our shared humanity and the tangible improvements we can make here and now. This isn't just about creating a new world; it's about recognizing and amplifying the beauty in our current one.

Chapter 10: Challenges of Change

Transforming society isn't just about drafting utopian visions or having intellectual discussions. The real challenge begins when we strive to turn these ideas into tangible actions. This journey of rethinking and reshaping our world to dismantle entrenched norms and structures is fraught with resistance. Change, inherently, invokes fear; most of us find solace in the familiarity of our everyday routines, even if they are flawed. Proposing fundamental changes to the very foundations of our community or societal operations can trigger deep discomfort and resistance.

For example, consider moving away from traditional religious structures. This shift isn't merely about changing Sunday routines; it's about challenging beliefs that have been ingrained over generations. It involves encouraging individuals to look beyond long-held doctrines to value life in the present, without the incentives of an afterlife. This often meets with significant pushback, as these beliefs provide comfort, a sense of order and answers to existential questions.

Moreover, fostering dialogue about these transformations involves more than just initiating tough conversations; it requires sustaining these discussions even when they become taxing. It demands listening to concerns, correcting misconceptions and sometimes standing firm against emotional pushback, which can be draining. You find yourself needing to balance empathy with persistence, and understanding with urgency.

One of the most challenging aspects is the inevitable polarization. As you advocate for change, societal lines are drawn; progressives versus traditionalists, the future-oriented against the past-bound. This division isn't merely ideological; it penetrates into communities, families and friendships, transforming civil discussions into confrontations and agreements into conflicts.

Despite these hurdles, persevering through them offers clarity. Each discussion, debate and confrontation not only tests but often refines the resilience of these ideas. Through these challenges, practical and workable solutions start to emerge, not just idealistic ones.

Thus, while daunting, these challenges are essential. They compel us to confront the core of our beliefs, and question the kind of society we live in and wish to leave for future generations. Although the path is rocky, the progress; each small step forward; is significant. It's about keeping focused on the goal: a transformed society where outdated, restrictive structures are dismantled and new, inclusive frameworks are established. This journey, though arduous, is crucial for building a society that embraces change and fosters a more unified and equitable community for everyone.

Chapter 11: The Battle of Beliefs

Let's look into one of the most emotionally charged aspects of societal transformation; when deep-seated beliefs clash dramatically during the process of change. This isn't just about intellectual disagreements or polite debates; it's about intense conflicts that erupt when people's core values and identities are at stake.

Imagine stepping into a scenario where on one side, individuals have clung to religious or cultural norms for generations. These beliefs are not merely opinions for them; they are integral to their identities and ways of life. On the opposite side are advocates for drastic change, pushing for a society that prioritizes rational and ethical considerations based on current realities rather than traditional or divine commands.

This situation is a powder keg of potential conflict, where discussions are charged with a raw energy that can be both exhilarating and terrifying. Each side passionately defends their worldview, not merely to win an argument but to safeguard what they perceive as fundamental truths about existence.

In exploring these clashes, let's look into the nature of belief itself. Why do we cling so tightly to our views? Fear plays a significant role; fear of the unknown and fear that foundational beliefs might not be as solid as once thought. Our beliefs shape our identities, telling us who we are, where we belong and how we relate to the world.

Navigating these confrontations requires more than sound arguments or clear logic; it demands deep empathy, understanding and efforts to find common ground even when differences seem insurmountable. Successful strategies in some regions include fostering dialogues that bring conflicting parties together, initiatives that highlight common values rather than differences and educational programs that introduce new perspectives, without outright dismissing traditional ones.

These battles, though daunting, can be catalysts for growth and understanding. They compel us to confront our deepest fears, challenge our assumptions and can pave the way for building something new and more inclusive. I share stories from real communities that have faced these challenges.

Some have found ways to coexist and respect each other's differences, while others are still grappling with these issues.

However difficult, these confrontations are necessary for creating a society where all beliefs are respected, but no single belief system dominates to the detriment of others' freedoms and rights. It's about finding a delicate balance where we can coexist not just side by side but integrated into a world that honors our diverse experiences and histories. This approach isn't just theoretical; it's a practical and essential part of forging a more unified and peaceful society.

Chapter 12: Resolution and Reformation

As we look into the societal transformation away from traditional religious structures, it becomes clear that this journey is not merely about dismantling outdated beliefs but about building something new, and hopefully better. This type of reform doesn't happen overnight; it's a complex and often messy process, marked by moments of stagnation and sudden enlightenment.

The shift from entrenched norms is challenging and naturally meets resistance. Change is uncomfortable, as people generally find solace in the familiar, even when it's imperfect. However, this resistance also catalyzes significant growth, prompting individuals to question their beliefs and assess whether these are genuinely serving their purpose.

Imagine having lived under a strict set of spiritual rules and then suddenly being invited to envision a life without these boundaries. Initially, this scenario might seem chaotic or even unsettling. But as you adapt, you begin to see a world of possibilities, not constraints. This is where real transformation starts.

In this new paradigm, ethics are no longer dictated by the fear of divine punishment or the allure of heavenly rewards. Instead, decisions are guided by shared responsibility and personal integrity. We transition from adhering to external rules to nurturing a robust internal moral compass, making choices that benefit both ourselves and the wider community.

This societal shift leads to profound changes across various sectors. Educational systems evolve to emphasize critical thinking and ethical reasoning, over religious doctrine. New policies prioritize human welfare and governments and institutions restructure to uphold transparency, equality and the common good.

This transformation is deeply personal. Each individual becomes an agent of change, actively participating in crafting a fairer world rather than passively receiving inherited truths. This journey demonstrates that resolution and reformation are inseparable; by challenging and revising our past beliefs, we lay the groundwork for a reformed society that aligns with our deepest values of equality, peace and mutual respect.

This vision for the future is not just about creating a more equitable society but about enriching the human experience, making it richer, more compassionate and inclusive. As daunting as these challenges may be, they are vital for developing a society where diverse beliefs are respected, and where no belief system infringes on others' freedoms and rights. It's a thrilling prospect, indeed, one that promises a future worth striving for.

Chapter 13: A New Educational Paradigm

Let's rethink our entire educational system to shift towards a paradigm that prepares individuals not just academically, but as well-rounded participants in a global society. The traditional emphasis on standardized testing and rigid curricula often fails to meet diverse student needs, focusing more on grades than on real learning or the development of critical thinking skills.

I propose moving towards a more holistic educational experience, integrating real-world problem-solving, cross-cultural collaboration and emotional and social learning, alongside academic achievements. A key aspect of this new paradigm is making education universally accessible. This involves breaking down barriers such as high tuition fees and the inaccessibility in rural or impoverished areas, as well as updating outdated teaching methods that fail to leverage technology.

In a future where every child, regardless of background, has access to quality education through global digital classrooms and free educational resources, technology plays a crucial role as a great equalizer in democratizing learning.

The content we teach needs to evolve beyond the basic subjects to embrace a globally minded and culturally inclusive curriculum. We should be teaching history from multiple perspectives, celebrating scientific achievements globally and exploring diverse artistic traditions and techniques. This not only broadens minds but also fosters a sense of global community and mutual respect.

Moreover, it's crucial to embed values like empathy, cooperation and respect for diversity into the curriculum. This approach prepares individuals to thrive and contribute in a world where collaboration across various divides is the norm. This includes project-based learning that tackles global issues like climate change or social injustice, making education directly relevant to real-world challenges.

I'm excited about the possibilities this new educational system could unlock. Educators would become facilitators of learning experiences and students would become active participants in their education, equipped not only with knowledge but also with a sense of responsibility towards the global community.

This reimagined educational paradigm is about more than schooling; it's about preparing future generations for a world that values equality, understands diversity and is committed to fostering universal brotherhood. It's about ensuring every child has a seat at the table and the tools to dream and achieve big, for the betterment of all.

Chapter 14: Policies for a Present Paradise

To transform our current reality into something resembling paradise, we must aim high and implement transformative policies across various sectors. Here's a breakdown of some ambitious yet essential policy changes:

1. Education: We need to revolutionize the educational system to focus not only on creating future workers but on nurturing well-rounded, critical thinkers. Policies should ensure that education is free and accessible to everyone, regardless of geographic or economic status. The curriculum should be global in scope yet tailored locally to meet community-specific needs, promoting global citizenship and connectivity.

2. Healthcare: Establish a healthcare system where everyone has equal access to necessary services without the financial burden. This system would prioritize preventative care, treat mental health with the same urgency as physical health, and focus on wellness over illness. A global network would allow medical advancements to benefit all, ensuring that no one is disadvantaged by their location or economic situation.

3. Environmental Sustainability: Implement rigorous environmental policies that go beyond mere rhetoric. These would include initiatives to reduce carbon footprints, expand green spaces and promote clean energy usage. Enforcing these practices at both corporate and individual levels would make sustainable living accessible and economically viable, fostering cities designed with green corridors and efficient, sustainable transport options.

4. Economic Equality: Develop economic policies that ensure wealth distribution allows everyone a comfortable standard of living. This could involve concepts like universal basic income or wage adjustments that reflect real living costs. The goal is to minimize the economic disparity, making societal prosperity achievable for all.

5. Legal and Justice Reforms: Overhaul the legal system to guarantee that justice is impartial, accessible and fair. Focus on policies that promote rehabilitation over punishment, ensuring that the legal process is equitable regardless of one's socioeconomic background. Strengthen community safety measures to create environments where everyone can flourish.

These policies aim not just to create a functioning society but to cultivate a world where every individual can enjoy a life of joy, security and opportunity. By implementing such comprehensive reforms, we set a foundation that not only improves our present but also secures a prosperous future for coming generations. This approach requires a deep commitment and willingness to make tough decisions, but it is essential for turning our grandest dreams into reality.

Chapter 15: Visions of a Fulfilled Humanity

We get to a place in this world that the definition of what it means to be human is no longer just reappraised but rather redefined. On our trip through the revolutionized society, I feel like we might just be stepping into something truly transformative – a world where every policy, every bit of actuality and sentence uttered in regard to the happenings on this earth are restructured and reformatted to reflect actual human welfare and human-becoming. You see, considering the proposition of this fulfilled humanity – it is not about creating an image of a place that's light years away or only visible behind the blurry glass of reality. It is about taking what you've so far believed is impossible, like liberation from the fetters of the past and a world where everyone actually has an equal shot at their best possible life and asking – why not?

I look at this reformed world and see the one that's education system is unrecognizable. No longer is it about brainwashing students into future workers, corporations or history museum displays. It is about shaping the young minds into critical-thinkers, compassionate leaders, brilliant creators. Designed to be lifelong, it does not end the moment the diploma is issued but is rather something you carry throughout your life, readily accessible to each one at any time and place, ready to adapt to the changing world.

And then the policies, oh, the policies in this reconfigured world. No longer is the focus primarily on the economy.

Oh and let's not forget the workforce. Here, work isn't only a way to put bread on the table; it's a way to give back meaningfully to society. It's about more than just making money; it's about love and purpose. The gig economy completely transforms and flexibility no longer equates to instability.

But it doesn't just start or end with the big systems and grand reforms. It's also about the daily interactions, the small acts that show we're all in it together. I'm talking about towns where everyone looks out for the other, where the neighbor isn't just the person next to you. I'm talking about the luxury of time to chat and eat together, which easily gets lost in today's fast-paced world.

And trust me; this vision is much more than just bare survival; it's actually about thriving. It's about understanding that every human being has something extraordinary to offer and that our differences empower us and not divide us.

I'm talking about a place where these skills aren't perceived as a weakness; that they're our biggest strengths.

Because the reality is that the future isn't about creating a paradise; it's about making sure that every person around the globe can wake up every single day and feel appreciated, safe and motivated.

That, to me, is fulfilled humanity. And I don't think it is just possible for us, we need it. As we imagine tomorrow, this is the picture that can point us in the direction to reimagine the future we build, ensuring that we stride only in the path that scaffolds a better place for us all to live.

Part 2: No Countries

In this part of the book, let us take a closer look at the idea of a world without borders – a world with no boundaries, where the world stops existing in parts and where humanity flows in one stream. the concept of imagining that the entire world lives under a single citizenship. How crazy is that? Imagine there are no imaginary lines on the map, no parts of lands separated by fences and walls and everyone in the globe live in a single citizenship. This is not destroying or disregarding our heritage, but it is transcending our past limited identities to embrace a new broader identity. A state of mind that makes us feel that we belong to the world and the world belongs to us. And in this global citizenship, we don't only share burdens, but we share fortunes as well. Let's find out how this will change our interactions with each other. It's not just tearing down physical borders; we're talking about breaking psychological barriers that made us feel like strangers for ages will finally disappear. The whole world will look more like a village or unified neighborhoods where we stay with our friends rather than neighbors. The places we live in will not be defined by our location; they will be defined by the projects we want to achieve together and humanity's values. In this section of the book, let's explore how we will be most united and be at peace with each other. How will be stop competing and start cooperating?

So then: why maintain the concept of nationhood when technology and transport have made the globe so tiny and our economies and environments are so closely interconnected that they are barely inferrable? This is the type of world described here; where cooperation and human kindness far outshine rivalry and contention and where all human activities are focused on every Earth-dweller's shared good. It's a positive spin, but why not aim high? After all, major changes always begin with a dream, as history has shown us. Procedural modifications follow after someone has dared to hope of the unthinkable and has then taken action to accomplish it. As we ponder the consequences of a borderless globe, the reader is invited to consider the numerous issues and multiple rewards that might come from such a dramatic evolution. When we begin to consider how different the new world will appear, we'll have to consider the particulars. How do our laws need to be changed? How do our people govern their capital, land and assets? How would everybody's views and statements be considered valuable and important? This is not a fantasy; it is a plea for a total overhaul of the industrialized world's foundation concepts. Therefore, please allow us to take into consideration how we can find ways to become a hive mind, where no one is an outcast and where we not only stay, but we also innovate together to ensure that the envisioned future is a safe home for all at this very time.

Chapter 16: Borders Dissolve

Imagine waking up one day to find out via newsflash that all national borders had simply dissolved. There wasn't much excitement, no commotion, but then a sort of collective exhale enveloped the globe, as though the world itself had been waiting for this moment with bated breath. That's the scene I wish to set up for you. It's pretty calm at the beginning. In the beginning, everybody is on edge, not really knowing what to make of it. I would likely be gazing out of my kitchen window with a cup of coffee in my hand, contemplating how the world that I understood had changed in the blink of an eye. You see, the first realization I get after the fact is the notion of how much closer we truly are than we appear. The lines on maps that once limited me from doing and going wherever I wanted, from calling my neighbors my own, all of a sudden seem so strange, so unnatural, so absolutely necessary. I take a walk around my neighborhood and notice all the familiar faces, but there is more of us now than there were yesterday. A man from across the line is no longer just a neighbor; he is also a comrade. The panacea and the trifecta all in one are overpowering. As I look into such a universe, I consider the specifics. Any airport can be entered, any border is just a bus or a train stop. No more passports, no visas. I think of all the traveling I could do to places I never believed I would see, meeting people I always thought I'd want to meet. The exhilaration is contagious.

Sure, I touch on the initial challenges. Economies adjusting, governments scrambling to reframe policies and communities learning to embrace a sudden diversity deeper than just the day-to-day tourists. It's not without its fears or hesitations and there were plenty of disputes to iron out. But there's always opportunity too – a chance to redefine what it means to be a global citizen. From there, I talk about how life changes in such a world with no borders. Once-national festivals begin to welcome the world and languages mingle in the streets. Children learn human history as an integrated whole, not chopped up into nation-sized chunks. I think about how heritage sites – things that belong to everyone – not just the country they sit in – might work. Then, I think about the more personal changes. Families once torn apart by immigration find it easier to reunite and friends around the world aren't just faces on a screen – they're potential neighbors. There's no alien – there's a friend you haven't met yet and communities become all encompassing. Finally, I think about the potential for peace. What happens when things no longer have borders to cut countries into? What about national armies, fighting wars about lines drawn up by old treaties and grudges? I dream of a world where resources that once went to holding borders go to holding back pandemics and climate change. The chapter closes with me back at my window, the coffee long cold, as I daydream about a world that might just work together as one vast neighborhood. It's a dream, sure, but it's a dream that feels a little closer than I remembered.

Chapter 17: The First Day of Forever

It happened. The first day of forever. The world woke up different that morning: borders erased, flags shredded and all those messy stripes on maps that told us when and where to place our love, trust and support; they all disappeared. Poof. As if humanity had hit the reset button on the bad parts of our history and overnight, political lines blurred together as we realized all those countries were just another leftover dream. The street outside felt it too, excited mornings breeze that smelled like birthday candles. It was hope; the smell of fresh coffee in my morning cup as I stepped out the door and took a sip. The city was a mess; a beautiful one. People everywhere: talking, laughing, some crying. The doors swung open and everyone was outside: tears of joy, tears of loss. Not a monument to the distinct separation of my Americaness and your Frenchness but bridges; languages were mixing like sunrise paints. And God, from the mix of colors and twined words, for the first time ever felt connected.

So I headed down to where the customs office used to be and nothing was there. The sign, being pulled off the front and replaced by a banner, read; "Welcome, all." Nothing poetic or profound. We were finally all neighbors.

The day was like a festival. There were food stalls everywhere and it was as if all the music in the world had fused into one beautiful sound; it was as if there was a new soundtrack to a new era. I danced with random strangers who felt like long-lost friends, had meals with people who, just the day before, may have seemed like my 'foreigners.' It was as if the world had gathered and thrown a neighborhood block party to welcome itself back to the fold. As the sun set on the first day of eternity, I sat in an expanse of grass that used to be a border patrol zone. Families picnicked, kids played soccer and two teenagers tried playing the guitar. The conversations flowed in directions none of us had the courage to take before. What next? How on earth were we supposed to come together and solve the big problems of the world now that we were not busy building obstacle after hurdle after wall after fence? I realized then that this change was not just going to mean erasing lines on a map. It would mean rewriting the unwritten ones that governed our behavior towards each other. It would be difficult, it sure would. The world wasn't going to turn perfect overnight. But for the first time in a long time, I believe we were all pulling in one direction. I lay back on the solid ground as the stars came out; the sky didn't look different, somehow, but everything felt new. There was peace.

This was not only destroying what divided us; it was simultaneously establishing what united us. We had a long time to go, a lot to learn. But late on that first day, I watched as parents packed their children in their cars, watched children longing for the day not to end, and heard the distant, echoing laughter in the darkened night and I understood: we had begun something that cannot be reversed that day. And we were up to the task, up to the duty, equipped to allow that day to endure forever. Since it was just that; that every tomorrow would be as bright as that day.

Chapter 18: Unity Amidst the Chaos

And so, the old borders started coming down. Everything was picking apart, right? That is what most folks thought when discussing the consequence. But, then, as I recounted, this period when it all appeared to be in chaos, unity started to grow out of the most unexpected sites. It was sheer madness at first. Picture every boundary you had ever counted on crumbling in a single evening. Lines that had stood for generations were smoothed out. People were disoriented, scared even, and rightfully so. The governance was rushed off its feet, trying to comprehend this novel existence devoid of the previous protocols. Still, something attractive was being concocted in the middle of the bedlam. People reached across those barriers for the first time. Without the unnatural frontiers of nations, we started viewing others were not strangers or aliens but associates. The tentative fear was shifted by fascination. Who were those who dared to gaze from the other half of the fence or manned the checkpoint on the other end of the street? They were not, it ends up, so distant from those on our side after all. Institutions and businesses began to grow and prosper. These were not reliant on territories or citizenship. Instead, they are about common concerns and interests. In a village bisected by a former border that no longer exists, neighboring couples collaborated on their bakery. The products of these operations – products that united national traditions in a means that no one had previously experienced – undoubtedly enticed people that had only recently peered across the division with apprehension.

And then there were the musicians who, with their instruments slung across their backs, crossed those old borders and allowed their notes to coalesce into something so much more. It turns out that music is indeed a universal language. From an impromptu concert here and there to transformed former checkpoints that opened up their spaces for people to gather and celebrate newfound brotherhood with melodies and movements, the experience was pure bliss. And let's not forget all the technology. With the internet doing wonders we could hardly imagine back in that old world, it was no miracle Albanian monks learned from Japanese students and developed new farming methods overnight. The online spaces; sovereign in their own right; they transformed into digital town squares of ideas where the rivers flowed freely.

Dozens of new recipes were tried, stories had been shared and debates had been made. Yes, there were misunderstandings of cultural contexts and nuances, differences in language and idioms, but the friction of learning them all was our new global citizenship toolkit. We knew how to compromise and how to understand and it turned out that understanding is the real language of peace and cooperation. But most of all, what struck me then was the human spirit's resilience. We did not back up in fear; we leaned on each other as a shared humanity to achieve something more. That old chaos, which was seen as the end of the world to some, became but a backdrop against which the new picture of human existence was painted. For now, looking back, it was not a disruption, but a cocoon; where chaos became our angel and our savior to tell us dream and fierce we will act upon.

Chapter 19: Crafting a Global Culture

This discussion, the idea of crafting a global culture, strikes me with how deeply interwoven and inseparable the entire world has become. I enjoy contemplating the layers of tradition, conversation and shared experience that can come together to form a whole. If all the individual cultures on the planet, each with their own rich legacy and distinct practices, could combine to create something truly new – and universally inclusive and accepting. It all begins with reimagining what culture means to us. It is usually the means by which we identify ourselves and our past, on a planet with no barriers, could be a fluid, continually rotating mix rather than a set, unmoving entity. This concept is not about losing the core of our individual spirits but rather about allowing them to breathe and intermingle, forming a dynamic cultural picture that is more inclusive and everyone has a stake in. Then it implies revolutionizing the method about how we talk. Language is a disadvantage, but it is also a channel. The charm of being able to communicate in thousands of different words is powerful, but the difficulties of using that range are only helpful. This implies there is a common second language for everybody in the future. Perhaps technology has advanced to the fact that there is no barrier to language.

And then there is art, music and literature – the soul of any culture. These, more than anything else have a way of transcending borders and reaching hearts. I imagine global art projects that demand collaboration between countries and cultures – works of art that blend various styles and traditions to reflect our common human identity. Music festivals, art shows and literary works – everything would be there to create this new narrative of culture, diversity and unity. And let's not forget food – a language of love shared by all. Global gastronomic trends, I would call it, that utilize cuisine from all over the world but in ways that do not merely merge together but respect the roots of the meals by innovating on them, blending across countries and cultures. This is how we sit at the same table and share the world together. And education of course. Schools would teach global citizenship from early childhood, orienting children toward cooperation, understanding of other cultures and love of the Earth as our common home. Forget about reading and math – this is about healing our children from seeing themselves as parts of the problem, teaching them to be whole and solve the planet's challenges. And what about new festivals, new holidays – what if we celebrated not only our national victories but human victories, milestones in our achievement and cooperation. Imagine holidays that celebrate science, peace, environmentalism, and every person across the planet stopped to remember how far we have come, together. And last but not least – the digital world, that would be challenged to be even more connecting. Social media platform designers would not only connect but educate – teach us about world cultures deeply and understandably. Virtual reality could bring us into the experience of other people – not just seeing, but living their lives.

But what does that mean for identity? That may be the deepest question. Creating a global culture is about mixing and matching traditions. However, we may also be reassembling who we are. The goal is to find equilibrium – to combine celebration of our heritage, with openness to the rest of the world. It's a wonderful waltz of past and future achievement and acceptance. Ultimately, creating a global culture is about opportunity and compassion. It requires that we accept how alienated we are and a better world is so much more incredible because of it. My mouth opens at the idea, but I remain optimistic. It will be a tremendous challenge, but it will also be an exhilarating one. The path may be arduous and tortuous, but the goal – a world united not by technology or politics, but by culture – is a goal I trust is worth the effort.

Chapter 20: Identity Without Borders

Now, what would happen if we woke up in a world where "where are you from?" has a different meaning altogether?: one where one's identity is not boxed in by the lines of maps. I have often thought about what it must be like when writing poetry for college assignment. How much of our passions and our sense of community will radically change if national borders are not a component of our identity? For starters, we will not be American, British, Indian or Brazilian; we will merely be human beings, part of a global village. In this image, cultural exchange is the standard, as opposed to the exception, reimagining nationality and identity this way is not an effort to dissolve what is special; instead, what is divided will be transcended. Maybe Diwali, Chinese New Year and Thanksgiving should all be equally important events and all of these cultural festivals are part of a larger tradition rather than individual items. Believe how our everyday encounters might alter as a result of this. No country means more local diversity than that of your neighborhoods. Your neighbor could have been born halfway across the world and the local community center would host music, food and dance exhibitions from every corner of the globe. Education will take a holistic approach to global history and culture rather than one that negligently emphasizes the casualness of shared human relationships.

Even our approach to global challenges might change fundamentally. Climate change, resources management and economic disparities will not be addressed by individual nations anymore but rather by global citizens. There would not be an "us benefit at their expense" policy anymore. Every policy and solution would naturally gravitate towards the entire planet's well-being. Additionally, what about personal relationships? Lacking national borders means that the concept of long-distance relationships would change because relatively speaking, it had been as simple as changing state lines today. Love, friendship and collaboration would become easier to develop since the bureaucratic nightmare of visas and migration laws would not exist. However, none of this means that our personal stories and heritages would be lost. Instead, they would be enriched in broader narratives of humanity. It means that we would be able to relate to someone from a faraway land even more because we share their values and dreams. In the end, our stories our defined not just by the places we are but by the things we experience; love, aspiration, struggle and achievement. The more we experience those, the more connected we become. Thinking about that, it is shocking how everything we do is ultimately defined by the lines on the map, lines that we ourselves drew. If we start changing them, some at a time, we might start viewing ourselves as the citizens of the world. And in this identity, we all might start thinking big, acting compassionately and truly engaging with the world around us.

So, in creating this new global fellowship, we're not only redrawing the Earth; we're reimagining what it entails to be human in the 21st century. It's all about widening our perspective, celebrating differences and transforming the world into one great home. Isn't it a joyful world to fantasize about – we are all world citizens and the whole world is our village? That is the notion that I fantasize about and the notion of how soon we are or have a long way to go before we can transform this imagination into our true wonderful world.

Chapter 21: The Universal Language of Humanity

Imagine a world where everyone spoke the same language – not just in words, but shared understanding, empathy and the minutiae of the human experience. That is what I am getting at here. It is an idea I have been mulling over or what I call a universal language of humanity. A language we can share without having to reference words – an understanding built on a deeper level than what can be conveyed through traditional language. Obviously, this is not English or Mandarin I am talking about – it is the language of our bond, our connection, our shared understanding of what someone else is feeling or hoping for, a universal worldview built on our shared values but seen through the lens of our most intrinsic hopes and ideals. I think about how our countries – our societies – our world! – could work together if we started to convey more about how we feel for each other through our primary languages, rather than fighting and arguing over what the perfect country should look like. The first thing which strikes me is how communication frequently breaks down not because of the words we choose, but because of the contexts and meanings we impose upon them. Each culture has its own context and meaning systems – and thus connotations – which can lead to us talking past each other even when we are literally speaking the same language. What if our children – from the earliest ages – were taught not just multiple languages but the cultural stories of every other group of people on earth and thus, the emotional contexts they use to color the world around them also?

Then you have technology. Technology is bringing us closer to a world in which language does not matter nearly as much. While translation apps and real-time interpretation services are excellent, they are still just a small start. For example, AI may pave the way for tools that do not only translate words but also deliver cultural context and emotional nuances. People from different backgrounds could then achieve a far deeper understanding of each other, giving rise to true global communication. Another thing to consider is the role of art in this language. The power of music, film, paintings or dance lies in their ability to communicate what words can't. Much of human experience is shared and humanity has a way of picking similar themes. And since words fail where feelings prevail, one can communicate with another even through a piece of art. That is, would the world be a better place if society prioritised artistic literacy as much as scientific or mathematical literacy? What if we communicated on a level that is an emotional one? Lastly but certainly not least, we can't forget the prominence of emotional resilience and empathy in this conversation. Empathy is as basic as knowledge, skills and stability. While empathy training is more than just feeling what others feel, understanding why they feel this way and how to respond appropriately is possible. Hence, education about emotional intelligence, conflict resolution and intercultural interaction programmes are also instrumental in ensuring that the world speaks a common language.

And, finally, I dream of a future where this universal language will exist and our world will become closer and more understanding. I mean a world where policies and international relations are formed not only on the basis of their own economic and strategic benefit, but with a deep personal understanding and respect for all cultures and all peoples. It's a really big dream, I know. But it is not only my dream – I am not the only person who dreams of a world that would be united not only by technology and economy, but also by empathy and understanding. The universal language of humanity isn't just words – it's a foundation on which we can build a future where we always understand each other a bit better, where empathy and cultural understanding aren't just desired, but demanded from every person in our global society. No matter where you come from and what language you speak, you deserve to be heard and understood.

Chapter 22: Laws that Liberate

Imagine how dramatically altering legal systems around the world might set us free. It is an interesting idea to consider, isn't it? We generally refer to laws as a series of limits and regulations. Don't do this, and you can't do that. What if our legally regulated frameworks were built from the ground up to promote freedom rather than restrict it? First, let's consider a world where our laws are intended not only to punish or curtail behavior but also to empower every individual. I'm thinking real legislation that promotes equality and can be accessed by anyone. Consider the fundamental human rights that many of us others take for granted and now envision those rights as actually accessible to everyone, no matter where they are in the world. Part of this idea is rethinking not rays; how do you think law is? It's mostly some politicians in a room, maybe some lobbyists, and after that, a new law is passed that we really aren't sure how it will connect to our everyday lives. What if making a change required the participation of everyone? And I'm not referring to legislation that comes up for a vote once a year; I'm looking for a meaningful, sustained conversation between legislators and the public, addressing local needs and concerns. This new system of legality would be designed to overcome barriers that have traditionally prevented people from achieving it. We could see laws genuinely putting an end to inequality rather than solely preventing discrimination. Picture laws that serve to ensure that everyone, regardless of where they stand on birth, starts their course at the same starting line.

Another element to consider is economics. In this world, the liberating laws would not just abolish personal rights, they would expand into how we interact with the economy. I see the laws create an environment where small businesses and entrepreneurs can succeed, breaking away from reliance on monopolies and creating a market with actual competition. Freedom of speech is another thing. It would be about the laws upholding the rights of the press and individual opinions, but also about the responsible discussion. It's important to turn people into both responsible speakers and listeners, meaning that they get to have a voice, but that it does not come from another person's expense. Another is environmental. These laws would not just protect the land, they would make so it pays off to do so. It feels that such laws would introduce incentives for the use of green energy, the laws to encourage sustainable practice and fines big enough to be a true deterrent. The last piece of the narrative is the role of technology in all this. I feel that it is technology that could make creating laws transparent, people know them and their rights are observed. It could be apps that send warnings when an area changes its laws, open spaces where people present new law ideas, and discuss them or even digital townhalls where the legislatures discuss the process of passing the laws with the rest of the people. In the end, it is all about seeing the legal systems as tools for growth and freedom. It may sound naive, even idealist, but to me, it is hope grounded in real opportunities and crafts that can make freedom and equality a reality.

Chapter 23: Economics of Equality

Stepping into the idea of an economics of equality, envisioning a new sort of economy wasn't just about tweaking numbers or changing policies; it was an entire rethinking of what 'equitable' and 'just' really mean in our society. I wanted to understand how such an economy could function without leaving anyone behind. At its core, economics deals with the production, distribution and consumption of goods and services, right? But in this imagined world of true equality, these elements transform. It's not just about ensuring everyone has enough to live on; it's about giving everyone equal opportunities to thrive.

Imagine a job market where your zip code or the school you attended doesn't limit your prospects. Everyone would have access to high-quality education and equitable job opportunities. This may sound idealistic, but it's not out of reach. Consider universal education that maintains high standards across the board and career paths that are genuinely accessible to all, regardless of background.

Then there's the issue of income disparity. In an economy based on equality, the vast gaps we see today between the richest and the poorest would need to be significantly narrowed. This isn't about penalizing the wealthy; it's about lifting everyone else up. Mechanisms like progressive taxation could ensure that those at the top contribute more to societal welfare, while minimum income guarantees could help level the playing field. Plus, envision a scenario where corporations are held accountable to the communities they operate in, contributing their fair share to the local economies.

Regarding resource distribution, it's a challenging area. In our current system, market forces often dictate who gets what, usually leading to inequity. But what if we managed public resources in a way that prioritized access for all? Community-focused healthcare, public transportation that truly meets community needs and affordable housing could significantly alter lives. These are not mere luxuries; they are essentials that should be accessible to everyone, ensuring no one is excluded due to financial constraints.

One of the most intriguing aspects of this vision was considering how technology could revolutionize access to services and information. What if everyone, regardless of their financial status, had equal access to digital banking, online education or e-commerce? Technology could serve as a great equalizer, but it must be implemented with a focus on accessibility and fairness.

The fundamental shift here is seeing the economy not as a zero-sum game where one's gain is another's loss, but as a cooperative system where success is shared. By creating an economy where everyone's basic needs are met, we unlock greater potential for innovation, creativity and fulfillment across society.

It's a grand vision, indeed. But remember, every significant societal shift starts with a dream. Dreaming of an economy where equality is not just an ideal but a reality is a dream worth pursuing. After delving deeply into these ideas, I'm more convinced than ever that although the path is long and filled with challenges, it is achievable. And the outcomes? They would be nothing short of revolutionary.

Chapter 24: Overcoming Old Divides

Let's look into the difficult, yet thrilling journey of deconstructing those boundaries that have existed for so long. It's not just about trying to think globally and act locally; it's all about discussing the intricate implementation of a world without borders, where we all belong to the same global community. However, understand me right: the point here is not just to remove the lines from the map. Oh no, it is much harder than that. I'm talking about inspecting and disputing the ancient and multi-layered boundaries already integrated into the modern social paradigm, forms and codes; or in other words, who takes the blankets, the largest cups of playground mud and the scepter. And that beyond confronting inequalities and privileges, this approach should include hearty conversations and heart-hitting questions about breaking the modern-world code. I mean, have you ever considered how deep you let these proper places nest into your operating code? We are all so enswathed in our economic, judicial and accustomed boundaries that eraser and redraw; it'd require generations. Thus, it is a kind of work that must be pursued by everyone, from the prominent politicos to local traders. Also thus, I elaborate the possible strategies to neutralize the disposition to resist such rewrites, as these require a particular angle and mood to be gathered and then monitored, rather than trying to preserve the old integral social patterns.

This is where education comes in. Education is a crucial first step to overcoming these old divisions because, through it, we can learn what caused these divisions in the first place and how deeply they affect us all. And by education, I don't just mean absorbing facts in a classroom; I mean expanding our perspective, understanding how we got here in the first place, and imagining what's possible when we come together as a global community in the spirit of shared humanity. I also consider the role technology can play in stitching these old divisions back together. In today's interconnected world, tech can either bring us together or drive us further apart. Let's explore how it can help us break down borders, misunderstandings and economic barriers, how it allows us to share our stories with people on the other side of the world or work with people we've never met to achieve shared goals. Finally, we consider the lifelong process most of us undergo to heal these rifts in our lives. It's a journey of personal growth, involving identifying and pushing back against our own biases and leaving our comfort zones to forge connections with people who at first glance seem alien to us but who at the core just want to live a good life. In short, it's an exhortation for change. This is a challenge to us. It's an attempt to upend the existing way of doing things, reimagine the structures that divide us and invite us to build a world that is accessible and equal for everyone, reminding us we each have a role to play. Together, we can build a better tomorrow for everyone.

Chapter 25: Stories from the Melting Pot

There is always a tapestry of myriad narratives which can be told to portray such a diverse and vibrant world without borders. National borders have melted away, as seen in this great social experiment in human unity, and all these stories woven together, are part of the same robust narrative tissue, portraying our common global culture. They speak to the universality and personalization of shared human experiences, which define the roots which water the plant that is our common future. However, out of all such stories, Maria's is my favorite. Maria, from her small village in Mexico, extends her roots to what was actually Canada. She brings her heritage, her flavors, her music and assimilates them into the local life. This story is not only about opening a restaurant where she serves traditional Mexican food. Rather, it is about how she inspires the local community to adopt life as a fiesta; every weekend, they dance and play music, mixing beats from all over the world.

Another story is about Ayo, a technological genius from Nigeria who later ends up in the large city once named Tokyo; the Nigerian uses the tale lesson to develop a new genre of manga loved by young and old. You can also tell Elina's story. Originally from Finland, the now community organizer travels to the busy markets which were originally Rio de Janeiro. Little expresses her story more than her ability to be a quiet leader, as she unites the different groups in the midst of it all.

Perhaps one more narration, is the life of Jamal who grew in a household of his grandparents who moved from the Middle East due to the conflicts in this region. They settled in what was formerly Italy and he grew up in the neighborhood where people spoke in Arabic as fluently as in Italian. Jamal grew up and became a musician. He combined classical Arabic musical scales with Italian opera in his plays and people came to listen to his performances. Citizens gathered at old town squares and listened to the songs that were much more than just music. These songs were a statement of the harmony of cultures.

Finally, there is my train of thought that weaves through this melting pot of formerly separate nations. I traverse from the former country to the former country, from one story to another and meet hundreds of others. And the most amazing thing is that everyone I meet is eager to tell their story, to share their national spirit and to become a patch in the unified quilt of this new melting pot. With every passing train and every conversation over a shared cup of coffee, with every festival, we weave a new reality and every nation provides a new pattern. These are more than just stories from the melting pot; they are confirmations that humanity can cherish similarities while keeping unique and, in this way, produce a common and beautiful reality cherished by all.

Chapter 26: A Family of Former Foes

Let us zoom in on how people who once viewed each other as enemies can transform their distrust and division into unity and friendship. It's about fostering understanding and reconciliation on a global scale, which is truly fascinating to consider. Picture sitting down for dinner with individuals who previously saw each other with suspicion or outright hostility due to their national identities or past conflicts. Now, they're passing dishes around, sharing stories and building relationships. This scenario explores how former foes can become part of a newly knit global family.

The setting is a small community gathering that could be anywhere in the world, involving people from places with historical tensions like Greeks and Turks, Indians and Pakistanis, or Americans and Russians. They start by sharing their personal stories, fears and hopes. Initially, there's awkwardness, with hesitation in their voices and a careful dance around sensitive topics. Yet, as they continue, you see barriers beginning to crumble.

I'm drawn to stories like that of a young woman from Seoul who reaches out to an older gentleman from Pyongyang, overcoming decades of political propaganda. Or a teenager from Israel and a teenager from Palestine who discover shared interests in video games and music, seeing each other as peers rather than adversaries.

A pivotal moment occurs during a group project aimed at community improvement, such as building a small park. During these collaborative efforts; planting trees, painting benches, laying pathways; they find common ground not through their governments' agreements but through shared sweat and laughter. They discuss their families, hobbies and daily lives, realizing their similarities.

As the day ends, there's a poignant scene where they all sit back and admire what they've created together; a new place for peace in their community. It's symbolic, certainly, but it's also a tangible representation of what can be achieved when old narratives are challenged and new stories are written together.

This exploration continues by reflecting on the power of human connections to bridge divides. It's not merely about political treaties and peace accords; it's about the small, personal interactions that weave into a fabric strong enough to unite us. This new family of former foes stands as a testament to the idea that our shared humanity is stronger than the histories that divide us.

This journey isn't just a story; it's a blueprint for healing. It's a call to action for all of us to find the former foes in our lives and reach out, not with a hand ready to fight, but with an open hand ready to shake in peace. It's about envisioning a world where we focus on building together, rather than tearing each other apart. And who knows? With enough people buying into this vision, maybe, just maybe, we can turn it into a reality.

Chapter 27: Common Ground and Common Good

My favorite stories are all about us; a diverse bunch of people from different backgrounds and histories; coming together to work as one. It's a narrative about the residents of the world, even those with the most differing pasts, realizing that those differences can be a strength rather than a barrier, all contributing to a more equitable future. Imagine a place where every interaction, every conversation, helps you understand each other better. This isn't just about shaking hands; it's about lifelong adversaries sitting down together, not just to discuss peace, but to actively create it.

These are real-world success stories, where neighboring communities that once despised each other come together to solve common problems. It's heartwarming to see what happens when people unite around their shared needs rather than focusing on their differences. One of my favorite examples was an effort in a small town to establish a community garden where individuals from incredibly diverse backgrounds collaborated. This garden became more than a place to grow food; it fostered the exchange of recipes, stories and traditions, cultivating not only plants but friendships and cultural understanding.

Another example came from a city where major corporations that were once competitors pooled their resources to tackle urban poverty. They invested not just for profit but to create job opportunities and housing projects, demonstrating how re-investing in the community can yield substantial social benefits. These stories showcase the transformative power of focusing on the greater good. Whether through small acts or grand initiatives, when we consider everyone's shared needs, miraculous changes occur. We're reminded that our own well-being is intrinsically linked with that of others around us.

As I reflect on these narratives, I'm struck by how simple acts of collaboration can bridge vast divides. We all have the capability to contribute to a more unified world. It's not just about planning; it's about acting. This isn't just about feel-good tales; it's a call to action; an invitation to recognize our shared humanity and to build upon that understanding. It's about deciding to step out of our individual bubbles into a collective space where every contribution is valued.

This isn't just theoretical; it's practical. We're prompted to actively engage, to see the humanity in everyone and to work together to build a society where we don't just survive, but thrive. It's a vision of a world where our differences enrich us, making our society stronger and more vibrant. Let's not just dream about this world; let's make it a reality.

Chapter 28: Citizenship of the World

Reflecting on what it means to be a world citizen, it's quite astonishing to contemplate a shift from narrow nationalistic viewpoints to a broader, global perspective. Imagine transitioning from a 'me and mine' attitude to an inclusive 'us and ours' mindset. This isn't about simply erasing borders on a map; it's about redefining belonging. It's about caring for people not because they share the same national borders, but because they inhabit the same planet.

So, how do we initiate this transformation? It all begins with a shift in our mindset. We're conditioned to pledge allegiance primarily to our country, which isn't inherently wrong. But what if we broadened our loyalty to encompass the entire globe? Imagine the impactful policies we could implement, from universal healthcare to equitable educational opportunities, if we truly regarded every individual on Earth as our compatriot.

This concept might intimidate some, evoking fears of a dystopian global government. However, my vision isn't about imposing a monolithic bureaucracy but fostering a grassroots, global citizenship. This involves communities worldwide collaborating, exchanging ideas and supporting each other in ways that transcend geographical boundaries.

Consider climate change; a global challenge that impacts everyone, albeit unequally. As global citizens, our responsibility extends beyond reducing our own carbon footprint. It involves aiding those most affected by climate change who lack the resources to combat its effects. It's about recognizing that an environmental catastrophe in one area can ripple across the globe, affecting economic systems and human migration.

Education is pivotal in this journey. The more we learn about diverse cultures and societies, the more we understand and appreciate both our differences and similarities. With today's technology, educational exchanges can span continents, allowing students from various parts of the world to share knowledge and cultural insights, thereby fostering a global classroom.

Economic reform is also crucial. Global citizenship means ensuring that the fruits of globalization benefit more than just a select few. It's about advocating for fair trade and ensuring that workers everywhere receive fair wages and work in safe conditions. After all, the well-being of each global citizen is interconnected.

Perhaps the most compelling aspect of global citizenship is the profound sense of belonging it cultivates. Wherever you are, you're not an outsider but a member of a global community. Your rights are recognized universally, not just within the confines of your home country.

Achieving this vision requires a concerted effort from everyone; governments, businesses, communities and individuals. It's a formidable challenge but one well worth undertaking. By embracing global citizenship, we're not just passing through the world; we're striving to improve it for all, crafting a legacy of unity and shared human destiny. And in doing so, we may discover that our collective hopes, dreams and humanity are the very threads that bind us together.

Chapter 29: Governing the Globe

Initially, the thought of governing the globe seemed overwhelming. How could one manage a planet with billions of individuals, each with their own ideas, cultures and needs? Yet, as I explored the possibilities, it turned into a captivating exploration. Picture a world government; not the type feared in conspiracy theories but a democratic, transparent one that truly works for everyone. This vision isn't just about crafting laws; it's about redefining leadership and governance, selecting leaders for their wisdom, empathy and connection with people rather than their lust for power or political lineage.

Imagine a global council composed of diverse representatives from various cultures and backgrounds, all working together not to further personal agendas, but to find solutions that benefit everyone globally. This council wouldn't be hidden away but would operate openly, with meetings streamed live, allowing real-time participation and influence from people worldwide.

Transparency would be paramount in this system. Every decision and law would be openly made and explained, with citizens able to engage through secure digital platforms, offering real-time updates and voting capabilities on key issues.

Conflict resolution would be essential, with a focus on dialogue and mediation that respects multiple perspectives, aiming not for one side to win but for sustainable, peaceful solutions that all can accept. This system would also prioritize sustainability, requiring every policy and project to contribute positively to the planet and its inhabitants.

The potential for innovation would be immense, with global resources pooled to advance medicine, technology, education and more. By embracing a truly global perspective, letting go of outdated notions of sovereignty and working together, we could step into a future where global governance brings out the best in humanity, making the world a better place for everyone.

It's a bold vision, but one that illustrates how with courage, creativity and cooperation, we could transform the way we live and govern on a global scale.

Chapter 30: The Peace of Participation

Let's look into the transformative potential when everyone has a seat at the table. It's a profound idea: when everyone participates, our solutions become not only more creative but also more just. Imagine how our world would change if every voice was heard; truly heard; not just those that shout the loudest or come from the most privileged places.

The concept begins with the simple yet profound belief that peace is not merely the absence of war; it's the presence of justice and widespread involvement in decision-making. True participation breaks down the 'us vs. them' barriers and fosters a culture where inclusion is the norm, not the exception.

Reflecting on history, we see missed opportunities where a few made decisions for many. In contrast, real changes have occurred when grassroots movements empowered the masses to shape their futures, crafting policies that reflect the diverse human experience.

Imagine streets bustling with engaged citizens, where town hall meetings are as popular as football matches, and community planning sessions buzz with innovation. Technology enhances this involvement, making it easier and more accessible. Digital platforms allow for voting on local projects, forums thrive with policy debates and direct democracy becomes a daily reality.

But it's more than providing tools or the right to speak; it's about cultivating a culture that values and actively seeks diverse voices. It's about leaders who listen more than they speak, fostering participation not just for appearances but because it leads to better outcomes for all.

In this envisioned world, government transparency is foundational. Decision-making processes are as clear as glass, building trust between the governed and the governors. This transparency fosters a sense of ownership among citizens, transforming them from passive observers to active directors of their community's destiny.

And here's where peace comes into play: When people see their input shaping their world, the frustrations that fuel conflicts dissipate. Feeling heard and seeing the tangible impact of one's contributions replace feelings of disenfranchisement with belonging and significance.

This vision of society celebrates civic engagement as the highest form of patriotism, where participation in democracy is as integral to one's identity as their neighborhood or language. It's a future where everyone contributes and has a stake, thus works harder to ensure collective prosperity.

This isn't just a dream; it's a feasible reality if we embrace the full potential of participation. It's the world I envision; a place where peace is forged not through silence but through the vibrant, sometimes cacophonous symphony of all voices united in harmony.

Part 3: No Possessions

This exploration into a world without personal possessions opens up a radical rethinking of our societal structures and personal values. Imagine all resources being shared by neighbors; there's no concept of "mine" or "yours," but only "ours." Such a shift could dramatically alter our approach to greed and personal gain, potentially redirecting our motivations towards sustainability and equality.

The elimination of personal ownership might dissolve many societal structures we currently take for granted. It's not merely a fantasy about a less materialistic world; it's a critical examination of the very roots of our economic systems and how they influence our relationships and self-esteem. Historically, many tribal societies thrived with shared resources, suggesting that the concept of personal possessions as a measure of status is a relatively modern construct. Could revisiting such models lead to a more equitable society?

Throughout this discussion, we look into practical considerations. How would our daily lives change if homes, tools and even artworks were shared? What kind of governance and technological solutions would be required to manage resources efficiently and equitably? These considerations extend into ethics, exploring how a shift away from ownership could foster a deeper community connection, reduce social inequalities and redefine our measures of success.

We also examine the psychological transformation necessary for such a society to succeed. Without personal possessions, could we cultivate stronger shared bonds and redefine fulfillment? Instead of aspiring for the latest consumer goods, might our ambitions shift towards enhancing personal relationships, achieving personal growth and contributing to community achievements?

By the end of this section, you'll gain a deeper understanding of the potential economic, social and environmental impacts of a possession-free society. In a world where everything is shared, our relationship with nature could transition from exploitation to stewardship, making the dream of a sustainable planet more achievable and intimately connected with our social structures.

This part of the book invites you to boldly envision, deeply question and consider a profoundly different lifestyle. It's about peeling back the layers of materialism that color our worldviews and discovering what truly matters in a society where equality and sustainability form the foundation of everyday life. Let's embark on this journey together and explore where a world without possessions might lead us.

Chapter 31: The End of Ownership

Let's look into the intriguing concept of a world without personal property. Picture a reality where nothing belongs to anyone individually; no "my car," "my house," or even "my coffee mug." Everything we use is shared, a drastic shift from our current understanding but bear with me as we explore this.

This idea might seem novel, but it isn't entirely new or far-fetched. Historically, several societies have thrived on similar principles, living and working together for the common good. It's fascinating to think about how we could adapt these ancient practices to our modern lives.

Ownership is traditionally about more than just possessions; it's intertwined with control, stability and identity. So, a critical question arises: How do we find security and form our identities without owning things? Our self-worth is often heavily linked to our possessions, which is a notion worth dissecting.

Envisioning a day-to-day in a possession-free society, we imagine shared spaces and resources. Picture a neighborhood where cars, tools and appliances are shared. You use what you need and then pass it on. This setup wouldn't just change our usage patterns; it would transform how we interact with each other.

Economically, removing personal ownership could catalyze a significant shift in business models from selling products to providing services, emphasizing access over ownership. This could lead to less waste, more innovation and a potentially more sustainable lifestyle, encouraging collaboration over competition.

However, such a radical change raises substantial challenges. How do we ensure fair resource management? What motivates individuals if not personal gain? How do we prevent exploitation of shared resources? These questions need thorough consideration.

Yet, thinking through these challenges also allows us to consider the potential benefits; reduced waste, less environmental impact and a stronger sense of community. Redefining wealth in this context means focusing on what we contribute to and receive from our community, not what we accumulate.

This thought experiment involves reimagining human behavior from a mindset of scarcity and competition to one of abundance and cooperation.

It challenges us to think about whether collectively, we have enough and are enough. While it's a radical idea, embracing this concept could pave the way to a more sustainable and equitable way of living on our shared planet.

Chapter 32: Collective Prosperity

Imagine a society where no one owns anything, yet everyone has access to everything they need. Picture a community where the concepts of "mine" and "yours" don't exist; houses, tools, cars, even meals are shared. It's like a large family where everyone supports each other, ensuring no one lacks anything essential.

This might sound unconventional, but consider all the items we own but rarely use: the drill purchased for a single project or the car that's driven only once a week. In a world where prosperity is collective, these resources are utilized to their full potential and are available whenever needed.

How would this work practically? We'd likely lean heavily on technology to manage logistics. Sophisticated systems could track and allocate resources efficiently, ensuring fair distribution. This approach would necessitate a higher level of trust and cooperation than we're accustomed to.

One of the greatest benefits of such a system would be the significant reduction of waste. Currently, much of what we produce is underused or discarded. In a shared-resource society, products would be designed for durability and longevity, benefiting both our wallets and the planet.

Moreover, this model promotes equality. The disparities we see today in education, healthcare and living conditions could be dramatically reduced. Everyone would have equal access to quality resources, leveling the socioeconomic playing field.

However, transitioning to this type of society would not be without its challenges. Ownership provides a sense of security, control and identity. Moving away from this could be perceived as threatening, requiring a major cultural shift.

The economic structures we know would also need complete transformation. Banks as we know them, mortgages and credit scores would be obsolete. The economy would have to be fundamentally restructured to focus on sustaining and improving shared life rather than generating profits.

Dreaming of such a society might seem far-fetched, but it represents a place where every individual contributes to and benefits from a system designed to meet everyone's needs. It's about redefining wealth not as the accumulation of goods but as the well-being of the community. This could be key to solving many of the social, economic and environmental challenges we face today. What a world that would be, right?

Chapter 33: Sharing as a Way of Life

In this exploration of a world without personal possessions, we look into the transformative effects of shared living on our daily lives and interactions. This shift goes beyond large-scale economic changes or legal restructuring; it touches the intimate, everyday texture of life without ownership.

Imagine a day in this life: You walk down a street where gardens, cars, tools and appliances are all shared. Need a car for a meeting across town? Take one from the community pool. Want to garden but lack the tools? Borrow them from a shared shed. And it's not just about borrowing; it's about contributing, too. If you're handy, you might spend a day fixing items for shared use.

This concept of shared living deeply influences everyday life. Homes transform from private sanctuaries into hubs of community and cooperation. Meals become shared events, with large kitchens where people cook for the community, enhancing both social interaction and sustainability. Resources like herbs are no longer bought and forgotten; they are picked fresh from shared gardens as needed.

Financial transactions evolve in this world. The need for traditional money diminishes as bartering and goodwill become the new currency, focusing on mutual support to ensure everyone's needs are met; from food to shelter. The economic pressure to 'make ends meet' is replaced by a collective effort to care for all.

Personal space and privacy still exist but are redefined. Individual rooms or homes remain personal sanctuaries; however, the concept of ownership blurs, particularly regarding property and common items. Your garden, while a personal project, also serves the community.

This shared lifestyle signifies a profound shift in mindset: from 'me and mine' to 'us and ours'. It challenges the ingrained notion that success is synonymous with material accumulation. Instead, success is redefined as the ability to contribute to and thrive within a community that supports each other's well-being.

The implications for personal development and relationships are profound. From a young age, individuals in this society learn to consider the collective good alongside personal needs. Children grow up with a sense of community responsibility, understanding that their actions impact others and that they are part of something larger than themselves.

The potential positive impact on mental health is significant. Much of today's stress and anxiety stem from financial pressures and the isolation of modern living. In a community-focused world, where these pressures are lessened and connections are emphasized, overall well-being could improve dramatically.

This vision isn't just about changing economic foundations; it's about fostering a culture of deep interconnection and mutual respect. It offers a glimpse into a future where we are not bound by material possessions but are liberated by our connections to one another, proposing a sustainable and fulfilling way to live together.

Chapter 34: Industries Innovate

Let's explore the profound changes industries would undergo if the concept of ownership became obsolete. Imagine a world without "mine and yours." The implications for sectors like real estate, manufacturing and services would be revolutionary.

Starting with real estate, typically driven by sales, purchases and rentals, we'd see a drastic transformation. Without ownership, real estate would focus on efficiently managing spaces for community benefit. Homes wouldn't sit empty; instead, they'd function like public libraries, utilized according to shared needs. Architects and planners would design versatile living spaces, adaptable to changing community requirements.

In manufacturing, the absence of ownership would shift focus towards sustainability and innovation. Products would be designed for longevity, reparability and reusability, eliminating planned obsolescence. Manufacturing would prioritize creating high-quality, durable products intended for shared use over their lifespan.

The service industry would also transform significantly. With the concept of ownership gone, services would emphasize experiences and maintenance over sales. For example, car sharing services hint at this shift; this model would extend to various other sectors. Why own a pool or gym equipment when you can access these facilities as needed? Service providers would manage these resources, ensuring they are available and well-maintained for community use.

This shift in industries isn't just about removing ownership; it's about fostering a system that prioritizes access over possession, community benefit over individual profit, and encourages businesses to serve the community creatively and sustainably.

These changes would also likely lead to reduced waste, more innovation and greater equality. The economy would need to be fundamentally restructured to support this new way of living, focusing on maintaining and improving shared life rather than generating profits.

This vision challenges us to think differently and act responsibly, aiming for a future where innovation is driven by the need to serve better rather than sell more. It paints a picture of a world that uses its collective resources to build an inclusive, sustainable future. Such a transformation would require a major shift in mindset from competition and scarcity to cooperation and shared abundance, contemplating real, tangible changes that could address some of our most pressing social, economic and environmental challenges.

Chapter 35: The Economy of Us

This exploration delves into the intriguing question of what happens to our economy when individual ownership becomes obsolete. It's about overhauling industries such as real estate, manufacturing and services, envisaging a future where business operations are based on shared resources and shared benefits instead of private ownership and personal gain.

In this envisioned world, imagine homes and workplaces not owned by individuals or corporations, but as shared properties accessible to everyone. This could lead to more environmentally friendly and inclusive urban planning, with more green spaces and structures designed for longevity rather than luxury.

Manufacturing might undergo significant changes, shifting from competing to sell products to collaborating to create the best quality goods for shared use. This would likely encourage a move from quantity to quality, with an increase in durable goods designed to last longer and be repaired rather than replaced, thus eliminating the throwaway culture.

The service industry could also see a dramatic transformation, with services like transportation, food and entertainment becoming shared experiences. Instead of owning personal vehicles, people might subscribe to a community vehicle service accessible as needed. Restaurants could evolve into shared dining experiences focused on social interaction rather than profit.

However, such a transition would not be without its challenges. It would require a complete overhaul of our current economic principles and a significant cultural shift in values towards sharing and community rather than individual accumulation. The notion of success might evolve from what one owns to how one contributes to the collective well-being.

Economically, this model could dramatically reduce waste and resource consumption, leading to a more sustainable planet. Socially, it could enhance community bonds as people collaborate for mutual benefit. Although it sounds utopian, it's fascinating to consider what could be achieved if we dared to redefine economic success.

This isn't just about economic models; it's about reimagining our relationships with each other and the planet, building a society where we're truly in it together. It's about creating economic structures that support everyone fairly and sustainably. While the feasibility of such a model remains to be seen, with enough will and innovation, we could forge an economy that meets the needs of both the community and the individual.

Chapter 36: Beyond Buying and Selling

Let's explore a thought-provoking scenario: a world where traditional buying and selling are obsolete. Imagine entering a store, picking up what you need and simply walking out without the traditional notion of payment. Instead, the entire concept of payment has been reimagined.

In this society, businesses don't operate on profit motives but function as community service centers. Their primary goal is to meet needs and enhance community well-being, not to generate profit. Consider real estate; without the need to buy property, the focus shifts from competition for the best location to providing sustainable housing based on community needs. Housing is allocated based on necessity rather than the ability to pay, leading to optimal use of living spaces.

Manufacturing also undergoes a significant transformation. Instead of producing goods to sell, manufacturing focuses on sustainability and necessity. Only needed items are produced, reducing waste and emphasizing durability and utility. Products are designed to last longer and are often reusable, aligning with shared needs rather than individual desires.

The service industry adapts dramatically in this context. Services like transportation, dining and personal care become shared experiences. For example, community vehicle services replace private car ownership and restaurants might operate more like shared dining halls. Services are provided not for profit but as a part of living in the community.

This shift requires a fundamental change in economic principles and cultural values. The traditional concept of success as accumulating wealth is replaced by the impact one has on community health and happiness. Economic transactions focus on bartering and exchanging services based on skills and contributions rather than monetary exchange.

Such a radical transformation poses challenges but also offers significant benefits, including reducing waste, enhancing equality and fostering a strong sense of community. It encourages us to rethink our relationships with each other and with our resources, moving towards a model where mutual support and sustainability are at the forefront.

This isn't just a dream but a potential redefinition of societal structures where we prioritize collective well-being over individual gains. It's an invitation to imagine a world where our economic activities genuinely reflect and support our community values.

Chapter 37: Community Core Values

Imagine daily life in a world where sharing and collaboration form the foundation of society. Here, possessions don't define us and the core values of the community dictate every interaction and decision. Let's explore what this could look like:

Morning Routine: You wake up in a shared home that feels like part of a hub rather than a private, isolated space. Ownership is about caring for surroundings as a collective responsibility, not because they are your property, but because they belong to everyone.

Mealtime: Breakfast is a community event. Food isn't purchased but grown and prepared collectively. People take turns cooking and sharing meals, focusing on nourishment and bonding over planning the day together.

Day-to-Day Activities: Whether working, participating in community projects or enjoying leisure activities, you notice the economy functions differently. There's no currency exchanged. Instead, contributions to the community; through labor, creativity or knowledge; fulfill needs and desires.

Resource Sharing: Transportation, housing and technology are shared. Have an issue in your living space? The community collaborates to solve it, whether it's a repair or a redesign for better suitability.

Education and Healthcare: These sectors operate on shared principles too. Schools are collaborative learning centers where everyone, regardless of age, teaches and learns based on their skills and interests. Healthcare is universally accessible, supported by both professionals and community members.

Community Living: Core values revolve around trust, respect and mutual aid. Decisions are made collectively, with every voice valued. Disputes are resolved through dialogue and consensus.

Personal Relationships: Without the pressure to accumulate wealth or possessions, people pursue passions and relationships more authentically. Friendships and partnerships are based on mutual interests and respect, not transactions or economic gain.

Evening shared Activities: As the day winds down, you gather with others to share experiences, plan for future needs or simply enjoy each other's company. Entertainment, arts and leisure are shared, often featuring performances and projects that everyone can participate in.

Personal Growth: Living in this society doesn't mean giving up personal aspirations. Freed from economic constraints, individuals are encouraged to explore and develop their talents, contributing uniquely to the community.

This society is not utopian but a call to re-examine the values underpinning our lives. It's about creating a system where shared resources and collective responsibility address social, economic and environmental challenges. It's a reimagining of relationships and societal structures, aiming to ensure the well-being and growth of every community member.

Chapter 38: The Commons Flourish

In a world where sharing and collaboration replace personal possessions, life unfolds with a unique rhythm and meaning. Imagine entering a neighborhood where all resources are shared, from sprawling rooftop gardens to tools and vehicles accessible to all. This scenario isn't just about erasing the concept of "mine"; it embraces the principle of "ours."

The community pulses with life in shared spaces that are vibrant and bustling with activity. Here, people don't just come to take what they need; they contribute their skills and time. A typical day might see retirees tending to a shared garden while teenagers manage a free bike repair workshop nearby.

Mealtime transforms into a shared celebration of connection. Kitchens are designed for multiple families to cook together, creating an environment rich with the aromas of diverse dishes and the sound of shared laughter.

Even the design of homes reflects this shared ethos, with spaces crafted not just for individual families but to foster interaction and mutual care. These homes adapt to the needs of their residents, encouraging a deep sense of community.

Education in such a society is experiential and driven by community involvement. Learning extends beyond traditional classrooms into shared gardens, tech hubs and art spaces, making education a dynamic part of everyday life.

Work also transcends traditional norms. Without the drive for personal financial gain, people engage in work that aligns with their passions and the community's needs, contributing to a collective good that enriches everyone.

Economic interactions are based on contributions and shared needs rather than traditional currency. Trust, respect and mutual support become the new currencies, with community decisions made collectively to ensure fair resource allocation.

This vision of a community built on sharing and collaboration highlights a profound shift in how we perceive success and fulfillment. It's not about personal accumulation but about enriching shared life. It's a radical reimagining that challenges us to think differently about how we live, work and interact. This isn't just a utopian dream; it's a practical call to action, inviting us to explore how such a society could address many of the challenges we face today, creating a sustainable and fulfilling future for all.

Chapter 39: Collaboration Over Competition

Just imagine, there is a world where the adage of the good old "every man for himself" is turned upside down. This is, of course, a society where cooperation and not competition are a priority, people come together to share, help and make common efforts to improve people's quality of life. It's like our whole life was transformed, our entire way of existence, into a caring cooperative on a large scale. It's not that people are struggling to be better than the one next to you or retaining a possession. It's about people combining the best of their abilities to build what none could do alone. And I'm not being unrealistic, I'm being reasonable; I mean, it's not just about feeling the fire and thinking of a better future, it's about understanding that teamwork makes us all more successful; socially and economically.

This is what it would look like in practice: Instead of each household owning one lawnmower, the whole community would only have to share one set of tools. Would it have a big impact? It would be a tiny little thing, but it would reduce waste and save costs, most importantly – everyone would fill a bigger sense of community and interdependence which is somewhat missing in today's society. Now let's think on a mass scale. A business that does what it does doesn't just want to make a profit, they also want to be a part of the community. Of example, they don't need to play their partners or see who can take something out of the other.

Once again, education transforms. Even from a young age, schools teach collaboration. Students don't compete to earn the best grades. Instead, they work together to solve problems as a team. The focus of the curriculum may move entirely to skills such as empathy, teamwork and general communication. These are among the most critical skills possible if collaboration is the only method to survive.

Socially, it appears unlikely that people will be under constant stress. Anxiety, which can be worsened by the pressure of competition, may turn itself off. When everyone is no longer competing for everything, whether it's a job, a house or a spot in the top college, people have more mental space to make lifestyle changes and develop healthy relationships.

Some of the advantages of such a change will also be economic. Innovation, for example, when people are willing to give or take a clue, is almost artistic. Barriers to entry in many fields may be lowered, offering entrepreneurs and small businesses room to grow. It's not a dream. The most significant developments and inventions frequently result from collaborative, not solo, efforts.

Sure, it's a significant change from what many are used to, with competition and individual advancement claiming ascendancy. Nonetheless, the advantages, which include some that will be discussed, are compelling reasons for considering such a transformation of our way of life. Ultimately, achieving this begins with defining success for ourselves and within our environments. The overall philosophy is to place the group's possibilities over personal gain. This could be a fantastic approach to address some of the challenges we face now since we must work on a societal level to achieve them. We must start by getting everyone's hands dirty if we want to generate a world where collaboration is the rule rather than the exception.

Chapter 40: The Holdouts of Hoarding

Envisioning a world without personal possessions invites us to consider radically different lifestyles. However, not everyone might embrace such a shift immediately, especially those who have significantly benefited from the traditional system of ownership and material accumulation. Let's look into how resistance from such individuals could manifest and impact a society moving towards shared living.

Imagine a society where all resources are shared and there is no need to own a car, house or even a coffee machine. This concept could seem liberating, but for those who view their possessions as symbols of success, this change could feel more like a loss than a gain.

Initially, there could be significant skepticism. Individuals accustomed to a certain lifestyle might fear losing their accumulated wealth or feel threatened by the idea of equal access to resources they had exclusive rights to. This reaction is understandable, as societal norms have long equated possession with success.

Addressing these concerns would require a mix of reassurance and demonstrating tangible benefits. Initiating open dialogues about the advantages of community and shared well-being over individual excess could mitigate fears. Educational campaigns could illustrate how a possession-free lifestyle reduces concerns about theft, maintenance or the societal pressure to "keep up with the Joneses."

To ensure fairness and acceptance, efficient systems would need to be established. For example, enhancing public transportation to surpass the convenience of private car ownership or designing shared living spaces that offer both privacy and luxury, could provide practical examples of the benefits of this new way of life.

Additionally, supporting the emotional and psychological transition from personal ownership to shared living would be crucial. Establishing community support groups or offering counseling could help individuals adapt, emphasizing the mental health benefits and enhanced social connections derived from sharing resources.

The transformation could also unleash creativity and innovation in society. With resources no longer tied up in maintaining possessions, shared efforts could focus on public art, community gardens and shared technological labs, fostering a vibrant, productive community environment.

Ultimately, overcoming resistance would involve demonstrating that the benefits of a no-possession society; like environmental sustainability, reduced economic disparity and a stronger community; significantly outweigh personal sacrifices. It's about crafting a narrative that emphasizes gaining a world of opportunities through sharing, not merely giving up personal goods.

Chapter 41: Addressing the Anxieties

In a world where possessions no longer define us, it's understandable that those who benefited most from the traditional system might feel apprehensive about shifting to a society based on neighborhood sharing. This transition is not just a logistical change; it fundamentally alters our perceptions of value and success.

For those used to the security of ownership, adapting to a shared system might initially feel like losing support; similar to a child learning to swim without floaties. There's an initial panic, a fear of sinking because the familiar safety net is gone. However, just as one learns that water can support you without floaties, people might realize that shared living offers a different kind of security and fulfillment.

Addressing these fears begins with open conversations. It's crucial to engage not just those who are enthusiastic about the change but also those who are hesitant. Listening to their concerns, understanding their viewpoints and demonstrating that there is a valued place for them in this new world are essential steps.

Education is key in this transformation. Redefining concepts of wealth and security to focus on community contribution rather than personal accumulation can help shift perspectives. It's about illustrating how this new system enhances lives, not just stripping away material possessions.

Introducing incentives can also ease the transition. Demonstrating the benefits of a possession-free lifestyle, such as increased access to resources and freedom from the perpetual race to acquire more, can make the change more appealing.

Support systems play a critical role in facilitating this shift. Whether it's through counseling to help individuals adapt or programs designed to teach new ways of living, providing robust support can help smooth the transition.

Building trust is fundamental. This new way of life only works if people believe they won't be left behind. Ensuring transparency in how resources are allocated, how decisions are made and how every member of the community can have a say, is vital.

Imagine a society where you don't own a car, but transport is always available; where you don't own a drill, but one is always accessible when needed.

This might sound radical, but it opens up a wealth of possibilities for stability, security and freedom that the old system of personal possessions does not provide.

Addressing anxieties isn't just about alleviating fears; it's about transforming them into opportunities for a richer, more secure life. It's about showing everyone, especially those who feel they have the most to lose, that they have an important role in a new, more collaborative world.

Chapter 42: Transitioning to Trust

Transitioning to a world where no one owns anything might seem far-fetched, but let's consider what it would actually require to shift from a society addicted to ownership to one that embraces sharing everything. Think about it: nothing is personal anymore; everything is shared. This change isn't just about relinquishing possessions; it's about cultivating a new level of trust among everyone.

Initially, such a transition might alarm many, especially those who have historically had more than others. It's one thing to share leftovers; it's entirely another to share everything you need all the time. The challenge then becomes: how do you convince those who have benefited the most from owning things to embrace this new way of life?

It all starts with dialogue; open, honest conversations about what's frightening about this transition. For many, the fear might be losing control or not having enough in the future. Addressing these fears directly is crucial, as it demonstrates that a community-based approach can offer more stability than the constant competition and anxiety associated with owning things.

Education also plays a pivotal role. It's important to teach people about the benefits of sharing not just tools and gadgets, but also space, skills and time. It's about helping people understand that by pooling resources, everyone actually ends up with more access, more freedom and greater security.

Pilot projects can serve as powerful examples, showcasing real-life scenarios where sharing leads to thriving communities. When people see firsthand that their neighbors are content without personal ownership, the concept becomes less intimidating and more tangible.

Ensuring safety nets is also essential. People need to feel secure during the transition. By guaranteeing fundamental needs like food, shelter and healthcare, we can alleviate fears of scarcity that might deter people from embracing a shared-based system.

Lastly, fostering a culture of empathy and cooperation is key. Celebrating acts of sharing and collaboration, recognizing those who lead by example and nurturing the community bonds that form when people look out for each other are all important steps.

This transition to trust isn't just about persuading people to give up their possessions. It's a comprehensive shift in how we view security, value and community. It's about proving that together, we can create a system that's not only sustainable but also more fulfilling for everyone involved.

Chapter 43: A Culture of Creativity

Imagining a world without materialism and possessions leads to intriguing ideas about the role of creativity. In such a society, creativity wouldn't be driven by profit or competition, but by the joy of creating and a shared spirit of innovation. Here, creativity would be an integral part of daily life, not confined by the need for commercial success or wealth accumulation.

Artists and innovators would no longer create to cater to markets or trends but would have the freedom to experiment and express themselves in groundbreaking ways, enriching society with diverse and dynamic cultural expressions. The collaborative potential in a possession-free society would be immense. Without the barriers of personal gain, people from various fields; artists, scientists, thinkers; could freely share ideas, fostering an environment where collaborative spaces flourish and collective creativity thrives.

Such freedom from material constraints would also transform education, emphasizing creativity and critical thinking over competitive achievement. Schools could become places of exploration and discovery, nurturing a generation that values intellectual and artistic pursuits more than material success.

Public spaces would reflect this new ethos, with community arts centers, galleries, workshops and maker spaces open to all, democratizing production and artistic expression. Success in this society wouldn't be measured by wealth or possessions but by community engagement, the diversity of creative outputs and overall well-being.

This shift would not only foster a richer cultural life but could also lead to significant advancements in technology and science, as unrestricted collaborative innovation becomes the norm. The societal benefits; enhanced shared bonds, reduced economic disparities and a greater focus on sustainable living; highlight the profound impact that embracing a possession-free, creativity-driven society could have.

Chapter 44: Sustainable Societies

Exploring a world where personal possessions are obsolete invites us to imagine a society deeply committed to sustainability in every aspect. In this envisioned community, everything from housing to resources is shared, profoundly altering our relationship with consumption and environmental impact.

In such cities, buildings are designed not only to minimize environmental impact but also to maximize shared living. Solar panels, wind turbines and green roofs become standard, integral parts of the infrastructure, supporting a shared energy system that benefits everyone.

Transportation is transformed into efficient, shared systems, reducing pollution and congestion. Car sharing becomes the norm and excellent public transport systems are preferred, leading to less crowded roads and repurposed parking spaces into parks and community areas.

The food system is revolutionized with community gardens and vertical farms becoming commonplace, eliminating concerns about food miles and pesticide use. People grow food locally and organically, not just for themselves but for their community, fostering a sustainable future where technology and tradition merge to ensure food security.

Economically, the focus shifts from personal wealth to community well-being. People's roles and jobs are about contributing to shared needs and individuals are valued for their skills and contributions rather than their financial status.

Education is tailored to sustain these ideals, emphasizing environmental stewardship, community involvement and creativity. Schools become places where students learn about sustainable living practices like permaculture, renewable energy and resource management, ensuring each generation is better equipped to continue this lifestyle.

Public spaces are transformed into areas for community arts, galleries, workshops and maker spaces, democratizing creative expression and making it accessible to all. Success in this society is measured not by economic growth but by community engagement, creative output and overall well-being.

This shift in societal values promotes a culture where creativity flourishes as people are liberated from the pursuit of material wealth. The arts and culture thrive as community projects become crucial social activities that enhance shared bonds and individual well-being.

While this vision might sound utopian, elements of it are already being implemented in small communities around the world, proving that such a transformation is possible. This reimagined society shows us the best of human potential, achieved not through the accumulation of possessions but through shared experiences and collective creativity.

Chapter 45: The New Wealth of Wellbeing

When you visualize a world where possessions and wealth no longer dictate your worth, you arrive at a beautiful concept: well-being becomes the new wealth. It's a shift from valuing possessions to valuing happiness, where the quality of your life isn't measured by what you own but by your sense of community and the depth of your relationships.

Imagine waking up in a neighborhood where the first thought everyone has is, "How can I help you today?" Instead of being preoccupied with acquiring the latest gadgets or a bigger house, people are more concerned about ensuring their neighbors are well-fed, supported and happy. This isn't a utopian fantasy; it's a practical vision that brings out the best in humanity.

In this society, the economy revolves around services that enhance life quality. Jobs and roles focus on arts, education, environmental stewardship, mental health care and community building, not on making money or beating the competition. This shift isn't just about being less materialistic; it's about solving real-world problems like loneliness, pollution and educational disparities.

Sustainability naturally follows this shift. When personal possessions lose their importance, production slows on unnecessary items and industries pivot towards practices that positively impact the community and the planet.

Daily life in this society is rich with shared activities. Parks are transformed into vibrant community centers with art classes, health workshops and public forums. Education emphasizes collaboration and critical thinking over competition, preparing children to contribute to the community's well-being.

Social interactions and relationships deepen as people become more authentic and less concerned with keeping up appearances. The community's support reduces financial stress and enhances mental health, providing a sense of belonging and fulfillment.

In essence, the new wealth of well-being creates a society where everyone feels valued for who they are and what they contribute, not for what they own. It's about discovering the richness in our relationships and experiences; a truly richer way to live.

Part 4: No Need for Greed or Hunger

In this part, we explore a future that seems almost utopian; a world where hunger and greed are ancient history. This section isn't just wishful thinking; it's a serious examination of what could happen if we reorient our societal structures and economic systems towards fairness and widespread well-being, rather than the accumulation of wealth.

Imagine agricultural innovations that allow crops to grow more abundantly than ever and advanced water purification systems capable of meeting the needs of a global population. Envision vertical farms in urban areas transforming food deserts into thriving sources of fresh produce. These technological advancements are designed not merely to increase efficiency but to ensure that no person must endure the pangs of hunger.

But this future is about more than just technological solutions; it's about a shift in the very ethos of our societies. It involves creating cultures where generosity is standard and social structures are inherently designed to promote sustainability and sharing. Picture communities with shared resources where the act of coming together transcends individual needs, ensuring collective sufficiency.

This narrative extends to redefining societal values, where personal worth is gauged by contributions to shared well-being rather than personal wealth accumulation. We discuss transforming economic indicators, moving away from GDP as a measure of success to metrics that prioritize the health and happiness of the population.

The chapter explores practical policies that could support this shift, such as implementing universal basic income and transitioning to resource-based economies that prioritize ecological and human health over traditional economic indicators.

This part of the book serves as a call to action. It invites readers to engage with a transformative agenda, using both existing technologies and developing new ones to forge a society where greed and hunger are not only reduced but eradicated. It's a blueprint for a future that is not only possible but necessary, offering a roadmap for collective action towards a world where equity, sustainability and compassion form the cornerstone of all societal interactions.

Chapter 46: Foundations of Fairness

In a world transformed by the absence of greed and hunger, the concept of wealth shifts dramatically from having to thriving. The measure of success is redefined not by individual accumulation but by the collective health and happiness of the community; a shift from "me" to "we."

In this society, wealth means having access to nutritious food, quality healthcare and robust community support systems; resources that ensure everyone can live well, both physically and mentally. Imagine living in neighborhoods centered around parks and community gardens rather than shopping centers, where work is not just about making a living but also about finding balance and fulfillment.

Healthcare in this world is no longer a privilege but a universal right, focusing on preventative measures to keep the community healthy rather than merely treating illnesses as they occur. Mental and physical health are given equal priority, breaking down stigmas and ensuring that everyone can access the care they need.

Education in this new society is holistic, designed not just to prepare students for the job market but to develop well-rounded individuals who value emotional intelligence, conflict resolution and compassion. The focus is on nurturing creativity and critical thinking; skills essential for maintaining a community where well-being is paramount.

Businesses in this world thrive by contributing positively to society. They are evaluated not by their profit margins but by their impact on community welfare and environmental sustainability. Success is measured by how much companies can give back rather than how much they can take.

Personal relationships also evolve in this environment. With the competitive drive to accumulate wealth diminished, interactions become more genuine and focused on mutual respect and contribution to shared well-being.

Technology plays a crucial role, enhancing life without replacing human connections. Innovations focus on sustainability; such as renewable energy sources that power homes and businesses without harming the planet and efficient food distribution systems that ensure no one goes hungry.

In this reimagined society, true wealth is defined by living well, where everyone's well-being is the foundation of community life. It's a radical rethinking of societal values, steering us toward a future where we all share in the prosperity of our communities and where caring for each other is as important as caring for ourselves. This vision presents a healthier, happier and more harmonious world for everyone.

Chapter 47: Feeding the Future

Feeding the future is not just an aspirational vision; it's a detailed blueprint for ensuring that no one goes hungry, combining sustainable advancements with equitable distribution practices. This journey begins with the integration of cutting-edge agricultural technology and time-honored ecological practices. Imagine smart farms equipped with sensors and AI optimizing resource use and enhancing crop yields, working in harmony with permaculture methods that honor and rejuvenate our natural environments. This approach isn't merely about increasing production but about enhancing the intelligence and sustainability of our farming practices.

However, having enough food isn't sufficient if it isn't distributed fairly. Herein lies the challenge of transforming how food markets operate, ensuring that excess food can be swiftly redistributed to regions in need through a sophisticated, real-time logistics network. This system would not only address immediate needs but also stabilize food availability during crises or shortages.

Localizing food production is also a pivotal strategy. Transforming urban spaces with community gardens, urban farms and rooftop gardens can turn cities from mere consumers into productive food sources. This shift not only reduces transportation emissions and waste but also improves the freshness and nutritional value of urban diets. Additionally, it reconnects urban populations with the origins of their food, fostering a deeper appreciation and responsibility toward food consumption and conservation.

Cultural transformation is equally critical. We must cultivate a society where food waste is as socially frowned upon as littering. Educating everyone; from children in schools to corporate executives; about the intrinsic value of food is essential. By reshaping perceptions, we can promote the view of food as a precious resource, emphasizing the importance of every grain and every drop.

Addressing hunger does more than satiate appetites; it nurtures minds and fortifies communities. By removing the anxiety and instability that hunger breeds, we lay a more stable foundation for societal peace and productivity. This comprehensive strategy looks at hunger through multiple lenses; technological, logistical, cultural and educational; to craft a viable plan that could genuinely make hunger a relic of the past.

It's a bold, ambitious plan, but with dedicated effort and innovative thinking, it's completely feasible to envision a future where hunger is not just mitigated but eradicated, creating a fair and sustainable world for all. This isn't just about feeding people; it's about nurturing a global community poised for greater peace and prosperity.

Chapter 48: Equal Shares

Imagine a world where no one ever has to worry about food deserts again, where everyone gets exactly what they need; no more, no less; regardless of their social or economic status. This vision, termed "fair shares," envisions a society where geographical or financial constraints don't dictate access to necessities. Picture community gardens in every neighborhood, state-of-the-art vertical farms in urban centers and advanced distribution systems that ensure everyone, everywhere, can access fresh produce and essential supplies.

This new world utilizes cutting-edge technology in logistics and AI to perfectly balance supply with demand, eliminating overproduction and waste. Everything from energy resources to basic food staples is managed sustainably, ensuring that everyone's needs are met efficiently and without excess.

Economically, this approach would also require reevaluating how we compensate different types of work. In a fair share system, every job, from teaching to healthcare to street art, is valued equally in terms of meeting the community's needs. People are guaranteed access to basic necessities, allowing them to live dignified lives free from the fear of scarcity.

This system not only fosters a new level of creativity and collaboration among people but also inspires a cultural shift in how we define success and fulfillment. It's about understanding that true satisfaction in life comes from what we can contribute to the community and share with others, not from accumulating more than we need.

This radical change in mindset could lead to a world where no child goes to bed hungry and no family has to worry about their next meal. It's a compelling vision of the future where everyone adopts a philosophy of fair shares; a world many of us aspire to see.

Chapter 49: The End of Poverty

Envisioning a world free from poverty involves not just alleviating immediate needs but ensuring every individual has the opportunity to thrive. This transformative vision incorporates cutting-edge agricultural technologies, advancements in AI and innovative financial and educational strategies to create a society where no one is left behind.

In agriculture, the integration of hydroponics, aeroponics and precision farming practices allows for the efficient production of crops in diverse environments. These methods use less water and space while maximizing yields, ensuring food security even in areas traditionally challenged by adverse climatic conditions or poor soil quality. Drones and AI further enhance these systems by monitoring crop health and optimizing resource application, reducing waste and environmental impact.

Beyond food production, technological advancements streamline distribution channels through AI and blockchain, ensuring that the food produced is distributed efficiently and ethically. These technologies provide transparency in supply chains, allowing consumers to verify the safety and ethical standards of their food sources.

However, eradicating poverty extends beyond ensuring ample food supply. It encompasses providing universal access to essential services such as education, healthcare and economic opportunities. Technological innovations like mobile banking and fintech platforms open up financial services to those in remote or underserved areas, enabling them to participate in the economy through small businesses and savings.

Education transforms through digital platforms that offer high-quality, accessible learning opportunities. These platforms leverage adaptive learning technologies that customize educational content to the learner's needs, helping bridge educational gaps and promoting equity in learning.

Healthcare advancements, particularly in telemedicine, expand access to medical advice and consultations through digital means, reducing barriers to healthcare access and allowing continuous professional support, regardless of geographical constraints.

The broader goal of this envisioned future is not just to meet basic needs but to empower individuals to achieve their full potential, creating a cycle of opportunity that fuels personal and community growth. This comprehensive approach to ending poverty focuses on nurturing the capabilities of each person and ensuring that the societal structures support their health, education and economic well-being.

As we advance technologically and socially, the dream of a world without poverty moves closer to reality. With concerted efforts and strategic deployment of resources and technology, we can forge a future where poverty is not just reduced but completely eradicated. This vision isn't merely aspirational; it's a practical goal that we are steadily progressing towards, promising a world where everyone has the chance to live a fulfilling and productive life.

Chapter 50: Hunger No More

In a future where hunger is eradicated, technology and innovative agricultural practices merge to create a world where every meal is an opportunity for community and shared joy. Imagine urban centers flourishing with vertical gardens and rooftop farms, utilizing hydroponics and aeroponics to grow fruits and vegetables year-round, regardless of the climate. These systems, which utilize mist or water environments instead of soil, not only increase production speed and yield but also offer the flexibility to set up in diverse locations, from urban rooftops to abandoned industrial sites.

Smart technology, such as drones and AI, plays a pivotal role in this vision. Drones monitor crop health and optimize water and nutrient distribution, while AI accurately predicts weather patterns and pest movements, allowing for preemptive protection of crops. This tech-driven approach maximizes efficiency and reduces waste throughout the food production process.

Community gardens evolve into more than just food production sites; they become integral community hubs that provide both sustenance and education, teaching residents about the growth processes and environmental stewardship. These gardens help localize food production, making fresh produce accessible right in the heart of urban areas, fostering a direct connection between people and their food sources.

The discussion extends to the necessary supportive policies for equitable food distribution. Transforming food aid, subsidies and support structures ensures that everyone, regardless of their economic status, has access to nutritious food. This approach redefines food security, making it a universally accessible right, not a privilege.

This narrative of a hunger-free world underscores the importance of viewing access to nutritious food as a fundamental human right. It paints a picture of a world where no child goes to bed hungry, no family has to choose between medicine and food and no community fears the aftermath of a natural disaster.

The vision is not just a dream but a potential reality, with profound implications for global health, economic stability and social cohesion. It creates a blueprint for a future where food security is guaranteed, leading to healthier populations, reduced disease and stronger, more resilient communities. This future is within reach, promising a more interconnected and empathetic global community, united by the basic human right to food.

Chapter 51: Tech Triumphs

In envisioning a future where technology ensures everyone has enough to eat, we see a transformative approach that extends beyond increasing food production to revolutionizing how we manage agriculture and distribution. This vision harnesses cutting-edge technology not just to produce more, but to make the entire food system smarter and more sustainable.

Drones become essential tools in agriculture, far from their initial uses, now employed to scan crops for disease and deliver nutrients directly to fields. This precision farming reduces the need for extensive chemical use, enhancing yield while maintaining ecological balance.

Vertical farms redefine urban landscapes, turning them into centers of agricultural productivity. These towers of greenery don't just save space; they drastically cut down on water use and nutrient loss, exemplifying efficiency. Imagine strolling through a city where fresh produce grows in abundance right where people live, drastically reducing the carbon footprint associated with transporting food.

The role of technology expands into the realm of distribution with the integration of blockchain. This technology brings unprecedented transparency to the food supply chain, allowing consumers to trace their food back to its source; a farm, a greenhouse or a lab; and ensuring that waste is minimized and issues within the supply chain are quickly addressed.

Artificial intelligence optimizes these processes, analyzing data to predict where food will be needed most and directing supplies dynamically to prevent shortages and surpluses. This proactive approach doesn't just feed those in immediate need but also anticipates and prevents potential food crises.

Moreover, the development of lab-grown meat represents a significant leap forward. This innovation promises to reduce the environmental burden of traditional livestock farming, which consumes vast amounts of land, water and energy. Cultured meat could potentially eliminate the need for livestock farming as we know it, offering a cruelty-free, environmentally friendly alternative that could transform our diets and food systems.

This vision of the future is not merely about employing technology for technology's sake but about applying it thoughtfully to address some of the most persistent challenges humanity faces; hunger and environmental degradation. By leveraging these technologies, we can move toward a world where food is abundant, sustainable and accessible to all, fulfilling the promise of technology as a force for good. This is more than a technological revolution; it's a new paradigm for how we interact with and think about the very basics of human need.

Chapter 52: A Generous Generation

In a world where generosity surpasses greed, everyday life is radically transformed into a harmonious blend of community support and mutual respect. Imagine walking through a city where every aspect, from public spaces to business models, embodies a profound commitment to collective well-being.

Public spaces in this society are plentiful and meticulously cared for, reflecting the community's dedication to ensuring that everyone has access to serene environments. Cafés and restaurants adopt pay-what-you-can models, making sure that meals and warm drinks are accessible to all, regardless of their financial situation. This is not charity, but a new normal, ensuring no one is excluded from basic comforts.

Businesses operate on cooperative models where decisions are made democratically, profits are shared equitably among all employees or reinvested back into the community. Success in this society isn't measured by profit margins or personal accumulation but by positive impacts on people's lives and the environment.

Education systems are reimagined to prioritize empathy, cooperation and community involvement from an early age. Schools become incubators for generosity, teaching children the value and impact of looking out for others alongside traditional academic subjects. Projects and curriculums are designed to demonstrate the tangible benefits of cooperation and selflessness, fostering a natural inclination towards altruism.

Media in this world reinforces these values by celebrating acts of kindness and community achievements. Television, movies and news highlight and honor selfless acts, helping to set societal norms where generosity is esteemed above all. This media environment helps cultivate a culture where positive stories inspire others to act kindly, further embedding these values into the social fabric.

The macro implications of such a society are profound. Economic and social policies rooted in generosity effectively address and reduce issues like poverty and inequality. With resources distributed to meet the needs of all rather than to accumulate for a few, challenges like hunger become obsolete.

The idea of hoarding resources in such a society is not only socially unacceptable but also practically pointless.

The concept of a "generous generation" characterizes this society, where community well-being and personal responsibility for others are not aspirational but the standard mode of living. Generosity here is not occasional but consistent, driven by the understanding that the survival and prosperity of the community as a whole enhance individual lives.

Such a societal structure marks a shift from a focus on individual accumulation to a focus on shared contribution and support. Here, success is defined not by what one has but by what one contributes to the collective good. In this world, generosity is the cornerstone of social interaction and the driving force behind a thriving, inclusive society.

Chapter 53: Value in Virtue

Envisioning a society where virtues like generosity, empathy and cooperation outshine greed and personal gain paints a picture of a fundamentally transformed world. In this scenario, core values shift dramatically, placing a premium on selflessness and community well-being above individual wealth and success.

In such a society, businesses would operate under a new paradigm. Their primary objective would not be maximizing profit but enhancing community well-being. Imagine companies evaluated by their social impact, where success is measured by contributions to societal health and happiness rather than bottom-line figures. This would foster an environment where corporations behave more like community members and less like distant entities focused solely on profits.

Education systems would also undergo significant transformation. Schools would prioritize character education, teaching children the importance of virtues such as kindness and cooperation with the same rigor and dedication as traditional academic subjects. The curriculum would integrate real-life applications of these virtues, preparing students to act as compassionate citizens in the wider world.

Media would play a crucial role in reinforcing these societal values. By highlighting acts of kindness and community support, the media would help normalize and celebrate selflessness. Stories of people helping people would dominate news cycles, promoting a culture where such behaviors are not only admired but expected.

The shift away from greed to generosity could be catalyzed by a new approach to upbringing, where children are taught from a young age that the highest fulfillment comes from serving and improving their communities. Such education would likely be supported by media and societal cues that consistently message the value of sharing over hoarding.

As greed becomes stigmatized, a culture of open generosity could flourish, transforming even the economic landscape. Companies might evolve into social enterprises that prioritize community impact alongside or even above profits. Economic indicators could shift to measure quality of life and societal health, rather than just economic output.

The ripple effects on society would be profound. Reduced competition and increased cooperation could lead to lower levels of stress and higher life satisfaction. Mental health might improve as societal pressures to accumulate wealth diminish. Community support systems would strengthen, making society more resilient to crises.

In this world, the definition of success would be rewritten. Wealth would no longer refer to one's financial holdings but to one's contribution to the collective good. This redefinition could help forge a society where mutual support and collective well-being are the keystones of all policies and practices.

This vision of a virtue-led society is not merely a utopian dream but a possible reality. It calls for a concerted effort to cultivate and elevate virtues that foster shared life and well-being, promising a richer, more fulfilling existence for all. It's a compelling shift from a world centered on 'me' to a world focused on 'we,' offering a practical pathway to a more equitable and harmonious society.

Chapter 54: The Gift Economy

The gift economy embodies a transformative shift from a market-driven system to one anchored in generosity and mutual support, fundamentally redefining the dynamics of how goods and services are exchanged. This model is based on the principle that individuals participate in an exchange without the immediate or direct expectation of receiving something in return. It taps into a deeper sense of community and personal connection that is often absent in the transactional nature of conventional economic systems.

In a gift economy, generosity is not just a virtue; it becomes the central mechanism of economic activity. Envision attending a market where items are offered freely rather than sold. People take what they need and give what they can, relying on a shared trust that their own needs will be met in turn by the community. This system strengthens social bonds, as people actively look out for one another, understanding that individual well-being is deeply intertwined with that of the community.

This approach challenges traditional notions of greed and accumulation. When community support reliably meets individual needs, the impetus to hoard resources diminishes. People feel appreciated for their contributions to the community rather than their capacity to accumulate wealth. The shift from individual accumulation to collective well-being could lead to greater shared satisfaction and connection.

A gift economy also promotes sustainable practices. As the system values sustainability over profit, it encourages behaviors that align with environmental stewardship. Participants might consume less and reuse more, recognizing that their contributions support others and that resources will circulate back to them in different forms. This could significantly reduce waste and slow the depletion of natural resources, bringing economic activities into closer harmony with ecological sustainability.

However, transitioning to a gift economy involves significant challenges, including a substantial cultural shift and a reevaluation of societal values at every level; from individual attitudes to global policies. The key benefits of reduced inequality, stronger community ties and a healthier environment present a compelling case for exploration and gradual adoption.

Implementing such a system can start on a small scale. Local exchange networks can serve as testing grounds where the principles of a gift economy are practiced within a community, allowing participants to experience the benefits and challenges firsthand. These initiatives can serve as models, demonstrating the viability and advantages of a generosity-based system.

Expanding these practices requires nurturing a culture of sharing and demonstrating the tangible benefits of a generosity-driven approach. This might involve community education, the sharing of success stories and the gradual integration of gift economy principles into broader societal functions.

The gift economy not only offers an alternative economic model but also proposes a profound transformation in our understanding of success and shared living. It suggests that our greatest assets are not the goods we possess but the relationships and communities we cultivate. Moving toward this vision, we could forge a world where the concepts of greed and scarcity are rendered obsolete, replaced by an ethos of abundance and mutual care.

Chapter 55: From Meager to Plentiful

In this envisioned world where abundance replaces scarcity, the fabric of society is woven with generosity and technological innovation, creating a tapestry of collective well-being and environmental sustainability. This ideal scenario leverages advanced agricultural techniques and efficient distribution systems, ensuring that everyone has access to nutritious food and that no resource is wasted.

Technological Revolution in Agriculture: The transformation begins in how we produce food. Urban landscapes are transformed by vertical farms that utilize aeroponics and hydroponics; systems that grow plants in an air or mist environment without soil, using significantly less water than traditional agriculture. This method not only multiplies the yield per square meter but also brings production closer to consumers, reducing the need for long-haul transportation and minimizing the carbon footprint associated with traditional farming practices.

AI-Driven Distribution Systems: Smart logistics that integrate artificial intelligence play a pivotal role in this new society. These systems are capable of analyzing consumption patterns, predicting demand and efficiently routing food from farms directly to community food centers and homes. This precision in distribution helps eliminate the age-old problems of overproduction and underdistribution that lead to both wastage and shortages.

Cultural Shift Towards Sharing: At the heart of this transformation is a significant cultural shift. The concept of shared living and sharing becomes prevalent, replacing the outdated model of individual hoarding. Community food centers become hubs of social interaction and cultural exchange where meals are not only shared but also celebrated. These centers foster a sense of community and ensure that no one faces the insecurity of not knowing where their next meal will come from.

Policy and Governance: Supporting this abundance are policies that prioritize human and environmental health over profit. Food is treated as a fundamental right; a shift that influences every level of governance and business practice. Policies are implemented to support sustainable agriculture, equitable distribution and access to food for all, ensuring that the basic necessities of life are never a privilege but a given.

Impact on Society: The societal impacts of such a transformation are profound. With the basic need for food universally met, people are free to pursue higher aspirations in education, arts and sciences. Health improves across the board, life expectancy increases and overall happiness becomes a realistic outcome rather than an idealistic goal. The societal focus shifts from mere survival to thriving, enabling people to live richer, more fulfilled lives.

This vision of a world where generosity and technology come together to eliminate hunger and promote abundance is not just a dream; it's a potential reality. It demonstrates the power of human ingenuity and empathy when harnessed for the collective good. By rethinking our values and the mechanisms of our economy, we can create a sustainable future that benefits not just a select few, but every member of our global community. It's a bold step forward, reminding us that with the right priorities, the future can be as abundant and generous as we dare to make it.

Chapter 56: Abundance for All

In this envisioned world where scarcity is replaced with abundance, the core transformation isn't just in the availability of resources but in the mindset of society. It's a profound shift from individualism to a collective spirit that prioritizes the well-being of the entire community.

Technology and Innovation: Advances in technology have revolutionized agriculture, making it possible to grow food efficiently and sustainably even in regions previously plagued by famine. Techniques like precision farming, vertical agriculture and genetically modified crops that can thrive in adverse conditions are widespread. These innovations ensure that there is more than enough for everyone, eliminating hunger and reducing environmental impact.

Cultural Shift: The deeper change, however, comes from a redefined cultural ethos that values sharing and community over individual accumulation. This cultural shift influences all aspects of life, from government policies to daily interactions. In a society where generosity is a fundamental value, the stigma associated with asking for help disappears and sharing becomes a common practice.

Government and Policy: Governments play a crucial role by implementing policies that ensure fair distribution and equal access to resources. This might include universal basic income, progressive taxation systems and regulations that encourage sustainable practices across industries. These policies help level the playing field and ensure that the abundance produced by technological advancements benefits all citizens.

Personal and Community Impact: On a personal level, knowing that the community supports one's basic needs liberates individuals to pursue careers and passions that truly interest them rather than being driven by economic necessity. This freedom leads to a more creative, fulfilled and productive society where people are motivated by passion and a desire to contribute meaningfully to their communities.

Education and Values: Education systems reflect and reinforce these values by teaching children the importance of community, sustainability and empathy from a young age. Curricula are designed not only to impart knowledge but also to build character, preparing students to be active, caring participants in a society that values collective well-being over individual wealth.

Global Implications: Internationally, this shift helps mitigate global issues such as climate change and economic inequality. As nations collaborate and share resources more freely, global stability increases. International relations are strengthened as countries work together towards common goals, recognizing that their fates are interconnected.

In this world, abundance doesn't just mean having more; it means having enough for everyone. It's a world where no one is left behind and the measure of a society's success is not its GDP but the happiness and health of its people. This vision for a future driven by generosity and sustainability is not only inspiring but also entirely feasible with the right mix of technology, policy and cultural transformation. It presents a hopeful outlook on what our world could become when we choose to prioritize the collective good over individual gain.

Chapter 57: The Riches of Redistribution

This envisioned world where abundance is a reality, and scarcity is a relic, offers a transformative approach to how we interact with our environment and each other. Here, the principle of redistribution goes beyond mere policy; it becomes a lifestyle, a cultural norm that permeates every facet of society.

Resource Allocation: In this world, advanced technologies in logistics and AI not only predict but accurately respond to the needs of different areas in real-time. Resources like food and medicine are distributed based on actual need, monitored through data-driven systems that track usage patterns and predict future demands. This ensures that surplus in one region can swiftly be redirected to meet shortages in another, essentially balancing the scales every day.

Community Integration: Cities and communities are designed with shared spaces that encourage interaction and mutual support. Housing complexes come with community gardens, shared workspaces and shared dining halls where residents can meet, collaborate and support one another's endeavors. These are not just places to live but places to thrive together, promoting an ethos of collective well-being.

Education as a Tool: Education systems in this world play a critical role in sustaining this new social norm. Schools teach the values of empathy, sharing and community alongside traditional subjects. Children grow up understanding the importance of looking out for each other and this philosophy is embedded in every other aspect of their education, from team-based learning projects to community service requirements.

Technology and Sustainability: Technological innovations are pivotal in making this abundance possible. From precision farming that optimizes crop yields without depleting resources, to renewable energy systems that power entire communities sustainably, technology is used not for profit maximization but for maximizing well-being. The development and use of technology are guided by ethical standards that prioritize sustainability and accessibility over corporate gain.

Economic Models: The economy itself operates under a model where businesses are evaluated based on their contribution to societal health and environmental sustainability. Profit is not the sole motive; instead, success is measured by the positive impacts a company has on its community and the world. Corporations act as community partners, playing significant roles in resource management and distribution and are held accountable by transparent, community-driven governance structures.

Social Cohesion: With a culture that values contribution over accumulation, social ties are strengthened. People see themselves as part of a larger whole, which naturally reduces crime, social unrest and mental health issues. There is less competition for resources because the system is designed to meet the needs of all, not just those who can afford them.

Global Implications: On a global scale, this model encourages international cooperation over competition. Nations share knowledge, technologies and resources to tackle global challenges like climate change, poverty and health crises. The focus shifts from national gain to global stability, recognizing that in a truly interconnected world, the well-being of one nation contributes to the well-being of all.

In this society, the old adages of "survival of the fittest" and "every man for himself" are seen as outdated, replaced by a new mantra: "together we thrive." It's a bold reimagining of our future, one that is not only desirable but essential for the long-term survival and flourishing of humanity.

Chapter 58: Guaranteeing the Good Life

This vision of a world where basic needs are universally met is truly transformative. It emphasizes not just the elimination of survival anxieties but the empowerment of every individual to pursue a fuller, more creative life. Here's how such a society might function and the profound impacts it could have:

Economic Structure

In this society, the economic systems are radically adjusted to prioritize access over ownership. Concepts like universal basic income or a guaranteed minimum standard of living could be implemented, ensuring that everyone has enough to cover basic needs such as food, shelter and healthcare. This economic safety net would be funded through progressive taxation, where wealthier individuals and more profitable corporations contribute a fair share to the societal good.

Healthcare and Education

Healthcare would be universally accessible, preventing illness from becoming a financial catastrophe for families. Education systems would also be universally accessible and geared towards equipping citizens with the skills needed not just to earn a living but to enhance their personal development and contribute meaningfully to society.

Community and Housing

Housing would be seen as a right, not a commodity. Community planning would focus on creating living spaces that encourage interaction and mutual support among residents. This could include shared areas for recreation, gardens for local food production and shared spaces that promote community activities and gatherings.

Work and Innovation

With basic needs met, individuals could pursue work that is meaningful to them without the pressure to accept jobs solely for financial reasons. This freedom could unleash a wave of creativity and innovation, as more people are able to focus on work that drives progress in arts, sciences and technology. Work would become a means of personal expression and community contribution rather than just a necessity for survival.

Social Stability and Crime Reduction

By removing the desperation that comes from unmet basic needs, society would likely see a decrease in crime rates. When people are no longer forced into corners by poverty, they are less likely to turn to illegal means to secure their survival. This could lead to a more stable and peaceful society where safety and security are enhanced for all.

Cultural Shift

Culturally, this shift would foster a greater sense of solidarity and collective responsibility. Success would be redefined not by individual accumulation of wealth but by contributions to the well-being of the community. Generosity and empathy would become core societal values, celebrated and encouraged from a young age.

Global Impact

On a global scale, this model could serve as a blueprint for addressing worldwide issues of poverty and inequality. International cooperation could flourish under the principle that ensuring the basic welfare of all is not just an ethical duty but a practical strategy for global stability and prosperity.

Sustainability

Finally, this society would likely place a strong emphasis on sustainability, recognizing that taking care of human needs must go hand in hand with taking care of the planet. Systems of production and consumption would be designed to minimize environmental impact and ensure that the earth can continue to meet the needs of future generations.

By moving from a focus on individual survival to a focus on collective thriving, we can envision a society that not only meets the basic needs of all its members but also creates an environment where people can truly flourish. It's a bold reimagining of societal structures, one that requires courage, innovation and a profound commitment to the common good.

Chapter 59: Prosperity without Profit

Exploring the idea of prosperity without profit offers a radical yet profoundly hopeful vision of the future. It's about crafting a society that values human and environmental health over financial gain; a fundamental shift from what drives many economies today.

Redefining Success

In a world where prosperity isn't tied to profit, success is measured by well-being and shared health rather than by financial metrics. It's about ensuring everyone has access to quality healthcare, education and housing. Prosperity means that no one has to choose between paying for medical bills and buying groceries; it means communities have thriving schools, clean parks, safe streets and vibrant cultural scenes.

Business and Economic Models

In this new paradigm, businesses operate on models that prioritize sustainability and social impact. This could manifest in cooperative business models where profits are shared amongst workers or in social enterprises that reinvest profits back into community services. Companies might compete on the basis of how much good they can do for the world rather than how much money they can extract from it.

Financial Structures

Financial institutions could evolve to support this shift. Banks and investment funds might focus on funding projects that promise social returns; like clean energy projects, affordable housing developments or education programs; rather than those with the highest financial returns. This would require innovative financial products and services that align with these goals.

Work and Leisure

With a focus on well-being over wealth accumulation, people might choose professions that truly interest them, leading to more fulfilling careers and a better balance between work and leisure. The concept of a workweek could also shift, perhaps reducing in hours to allow more time for personal development, family and community engagement.

Cultural Shift

Culturally, this shift requires a significant change in mindset. It calls for valuing collaboration and generosity more highly than competition and accumulation. Education systems would play a crucial role in fostering this mindset from an early age, teaching children about empathy, community responsibility and environmental stewardship.

Potential Challenges

Transitioning to a profit-less prosperity model would not be without challenges. It requires robust policy frameworks, global cooperation and perhaps most dauntingly, a widespread cultural shift in values. There would be resistance from those who benefit most from the current system, as well as skepticism about the feasibility of such a change.

Implementation

To begin moving towards this ideal, small-scale experiments in community living, cooperative business models and local currencies could serve as test beds, demonstrating the viability of these ideas. Policy initiatives like universal basic income trials and expanded public services could also help ease the transition by providing safety nets as society restructures.

Conclusion

While utopian, the concept of prosperity without profit is grounded in a deep understanding of the potential for human and technological advancement to serve broader goals than mere financial accumulation. It offers a blueprint for a sustainable, equitable future that prioritizes the well-being of all citizens and the planet. As we face global challenges like climate change, inequality and health crises, this vision provides not just hope but a practical path forward that redefines what it means to live well in the 21st century.

Chapter 60: Achievements in Altruism

Our vision beautifully captures how a society could evolve when freed from the constraints of basic survival concerns. This new foundation could truly transform our collective aspirations and achievements.

Altruism as a Way of Life

In a world where basic needs are universally met, altruism could become the new norm, deeply embedded in the cultural fabric of society. With the absence of survival anxiety, individuals might find themselves more inclined to dedicate their time and resources to helping others and contributing positively to their communities. This could manifest in myriad ways; from local initiatives like community gardens and educational programs to larger-scale projects aimed at tackling global issues.

Innovation and Creativity Unleashed

The freedom from financial constraints and the necessity of working merely to survive could lead to an explosion of creativity and innovation. In academia and research, this could mean pursuing studies that aim to solve long-term societal issues rather than projects dictated by profit margins. In the arts, creatives could explore and express without the pressure to commercialize their work, potentially leading to a new era of cultural richness and diversity.

Redefining Success

This societal transformation could also redefine what it means to be successful. Success might no longer be measured by wealth or status but by one's contributions to community welfare and global advancements. The esteem of individuals could be based on their impact and service, reshaping social dynamics and hierarchies in profound ways.

Mental Health Renaissance

The mental health benefits of such a society could be revolutionary. Removing the constant stress of financial survival would likely decrease rates of anxiety and depression, freeing individuals to pursue fulfillment in more personal and community-oriented ways. This could foster a more empathetic society where mental well-being is not just an individual responsibility but a shared goal.

Sustainable and Ethical Progress

With a shift towards altruism, sustainability might become a cornerstone of innovation and production. Companies and individuals alike could prioritize the environmental and social impact of their actions, leading to more responsible and sustainable living practices that benefit the entire planet.

Challenges and Considerations

Transitioning to such a society would not be without its challenges. It would require vast changes in policy, economic restructuring and perhaps most importantly, a significant cultural shift in values. However, the potential benefits; a healthier, more equitable and cohesive society; could far outweigh the hurdles.

This vision of a future shaped by altruism and universal security is not only inspiring but also a call to action. It prompts us to consider what steps can be taken today to lay the groundwork for such transformative changes. It's a compelling exploration of how deeply societal structures impact individual and collective well-being and how altering these structures could unlock unprecedented human potential.

Part 5: All People Living Life in Peace

In this part, we reach the pinnacle of what may sound like every person's daydream world today. It is the world where worldwide peace is no longer a fleeting wish that people toss out to the universe. But, it is an actual, achievable concept using tangible methods. A world without military structures, once again, the thing of the past dismantled entirely. Instead, our investments don't go into weapons or tools for war but ways to avoid it and solve problems and mutual understanding across every border. In this section, we will consider what revolution might drastically make a difference is if it happened and we can assure you that it could. We will discard the old tools of war and substitute with new tools for peace. Remember, these are no longer temporary patches and sanctions for harmonious, but permanent solutions for international and internal philosophy. This section aims to completely disrupt your notions of reliance and reframe the narrative you've long accepted. For a second, assume there is such a utopia where the globe lives in dialogue rather than explosion and harmony instead of a decline. How dramatically the power dynamics in your life have changed. How much more have you achieved had all people lived free from the tension of war? Moving forward has never felt so real. Once again, we will tackle the possibility in this section. How on earth does a world with no armies and weapons function? How can a society reimagine their budgets, policies and national identities, knowing that protection is not militaries but stable welfare and human health? This part not only asks the questions addressed but also proposal frameworks based on paradigms and illustrations.

We investigate instances from the past when historical premises of disarmament or diplomatic negotiations have resulted in greater success and use lessons learned from peace teachings by activists and peacekeeping bodies and organizations to make the point that sustainable peace in a practical achievement, not just an ideal. We interview political experts, peacemakers and community leaders to present a picture in which it is not merely a fiction, but something real. Each story, a single example of a vision where humanity not only avoids conflict but is capable of achieving growth and adaptation without it, can be considered as a possibility of immortality. It is also a challenge to every one of us, a critique on our contribution to this agenda. How do we promote or prevent peace in the world? Do we address this problem only when a dramatic event, such as a terrorist attack, a war conflict or an armed coup, takes place nearby or do we remain the Thanksgiving citizens with no real consciousness as to what is happening in other struggling corners of the Earth? These are the issues that everyone of us is to ponder today. Your role revives our security. How do you imagine it? Would you like to see yourself as a secure citizen, living in peace and tranquility or as a part of a universal nation threatened with elimination and violence? From the way you answer this question depends your relationship with yourself. And the book can help you deal with the problem.

This part of the book not only outlines such a utopic picture but also gives the path for achieving it. It erases the old legends according to which conflict is unavoidable and substitutes them with a new legend of hope and collaboration and long-lasting peace. This segment is a reason to dream but also to act with aspiration and determination, to become an example of a movement that is not bound by space or culture but by strive and persistence to ensure that future generations will define the future as a time of peace and justice for all. Therefore, let's proceed with the way together; let's cast the challenge with preperceived fears and dreams for a future where every human can lives peacefully. Let this be a mirror of reality and a hope for the future.

Chapter 61: The Last War Ends

Imagine a world where the drums of war have fallen silent forever. That's the world I dream of; a world in which the last war has recently come to an end. And not to the last bang; everyone simultaneously laid down their weapons and went home, never again wielding them against each other. It's not just a matter of conflict; it's a fundamental shift in society's ways. But how could that be the case? It all began with the world's major powers finally reaching a unanimous conclusion: the loss of a war is always irreparable. This revelation was not made in one night. It took all of human history, tens of decades of warfare and hundreds of years to reach this point. It all seems to have been enough. And it's the people of Earth, tired of seeing their loved ones and neighbors sent into battle against each other due to conflict he hasn't started, that unanimously demand to end it. And among those who went to kill, too, there are many who did not return. And now, all across the planet, places that once spent billions on weaponry have ceased to exist. Instead, there's now only healing and renovation. What once had been military facilities are now new schools. The technology and science that previously took the toll on human lives are now focused on saving them. Economies that depended on military aid are now thriving from peaceful corporations. And diplomacy is the preferred weapon of choice for everyone, soldiers, citizens, generals. With discussions, not menaces, any issues are addressed. Nor does anyone want to win. They want to help each other because everyone has realized the formation of an isolated winner in a global community; we're all losers. And that was the precursor of the last major struggle. But since all of the countries were officially allied, no such issue arose. They were corrected even more quickly and successfully. And humanity united, because humanity is one species on one little rock in a vast empty night sky. Now, everyone works alongside every other to keep their neighbours close, not to combat them. When environmental concerns threaten the planet, nations have united and enacted laws requiring the country's successful conduct. And now, everyone understands no one is behind whose ideas everyone aspires to peace.

Chapter 62: Disarming the World

Disarming the world? It may seem somewhat of a far-flung dream at first, but let's stop for a second and think whether it is. Imagine for a second that one morning you wake up and the headlines no longer scream of conflicts and war, but rather announce to the world that nations have decided to put down their weapons and sign peace treaties. It is not just the lack of military might; it's the possibilities and the infinite potential that open up once we stop spending most of our energy on protecting ourselves from each other. Most notably, it is . The financial aspect is mind-blowing. We all know how much money – billions if not trillions – yearly pour into the fangs of military industrial complexes all around the world. Then how does that money being poured into education and healthcare and clean energy sound? Although that may sound like redistribution, it really is something of a revolution – a shift in national values with massive repercussions for everyone's future. The environmental impact cannot be overstated – less military activity equals fewer pollutants in the atmosphere, as military operations remain one of the biggest reason for carbon emissions and other forms of pollution. What the world would look like with less of it ? The skies would be blue again, the oceans crystal clear and humanity may at least have a chance to address the problem of pollution. Everyone gains from disarmament, not just the ones who make peace. The ramifications are huge from a cultural angle. Just think about the stories we will be able to tell. Nations that used to be too people and nations that only chose to be a formidable presence may suddenly be known for peace initiatives and programs. People would stop confusion the world with the phrases 'worldwide conflicts' – just think of the movies and books we'll inevitably read. It's about more than switching passive aggression with active fighting – it's a complete shift in how countries view themselves. Socially, coming to an agreement on disarmament will mean massive change. Your neighborhood would no longer be associated with cultural hubs of military might. All those military bases whose impact on their local communities was more detrimental than positive? They would all be shut down . Because that's how societies look to other societies, right? There would be no more Leicester City and Manchester City – there would only be England. Egypt and Israel would work together to counteract the increasing desertification of the region. It's not all roses, of course. It's also about creating and developing trust between nations and other mechanisms to keep everyone on the same page. It's about empowering and creating international organizations that won't just keep an eye on disarmament but work to promote cooperation in lots of different ways. So sure, the idea of disarming the world may sound somewhat hippie, but it is not at all out of the question. And even the possible benefits are more than enough to make it worth it. We don't have to stop at imagining the world where we've stopped defending ourselves from each other. We can try devising a plan to get there – one small step at a time.

Chapter 63: Monuments of Militarism

As much as the concept of global disarmament is exciting, I find it fascinating to think about the numerous monumental military structures and monuments that have offered a symbol of power and defense across the globe. What happens to the monumental structures that housed armies, once we no longer need them? A mars where the barracks are empty and the hangars have fallen into a deafening silence. Decommissioned tanks sat quietly and mediums of what had once been a platform for war. It is such a colossal shift, turning war-centric places into centers for peace and community. For instance, an abandoned airbase has become a vast solar farm and the vast track of lands around it was turned into a place where generations play, have picnics and enjoy concerts on end and into the night. Or, the old battleships that once roamed the seas for the very purpose of waging battle have now sat silent and permanently docked turn into a museum or a cultural landmark, where people learn about war to foster peace, not indulge or glorify hostility. Other than serving as a physical record of our old forms of aggression, militarism memorializes could be tools of peace and justice. The steel that once used to fortify bunkers and command centers used to build homes and community center's, turning war tools into tools for enabling peace and prosperity. The vast track of lands and compound occupied by the bases turn into wildlife sanctuaries, schools or agricultural lands to offer food to feed nations and even the world. It is as much about a cultural and psychological revolution as physical transfiguration. This is a statement of advancing and securing lasting peace.

Chapter 64: Peacekeepers Prevail

When traditional warfare is a thing of the past, new heroes emerge in the absence of money; peacekeepers. These are no ordinary soldiers; they are courageous ones who enter the battlefields but not with weapons. They bring alongside them mercy, compassion and an unwavering commitment to solving disputes solely through dialogue and negotiation. Picture a squad of weapons masters who have been taught the infinite facets of military strategy. Individuals who have come from a range of professions – psychologists, diplomats, educators – some have even worked in the army and been on the battlefield, now fully devoted to the cause of reconciliation. They must avoid disputes from escalating and cure the sickness that rips them apart. This vision of a peacekeeping crusade is not purely an ideal but a fact. Current international peace organizations are working in full swing and are no longer on the stage; they are at the mediator's desk settling negotiations for belligerent parties. They have a giant round desk and sit everybody who has expected to express their dissatisfaction but has never been able to do so openly and without fear. In the result, there is only mutual respect and understanding of the one remaining aspiration – a peaceful lifestyle. And their primary success is that they strive to understand why these claims to one another emerged in this context and this precisely. They genuinely presume that others can understand the treatment.

Yet, ending wars is not the only added value of this innovative approach to peacekeeping. Peacekeepers on the ground make it possible to rebuild life in communities torn and devastated by conflict. They build schools and factories, promote economic opportunities and develop local governance systems that make peace their core priority. Lastly, they bring hope to places that have known only despair for too long. One of the most magnificent features of this new era is cooperation on a global scale. Countries from all over the world, as well as organizations, take part in the peacekeeping operations, recognizing that peace in one region also enhances the global security environment. Moreover, local people are now more actively engaged in peacekeeping – thanks to the new systems developing by peacekeepers, people within the country are trained to maintain peace and develop it further. Finally, modern-day peacekeepers are creating a culture of peace that will ideally make wars and conflicts a thing of the past. Through their work, they have instilled confidence that if we devote all necessary resources, hard work and dedication to it, we can reduce wars and create a livable world for generations to come. This undertaking is colossal and the road is full of failures and losses. However, these people motivated by peace, progress and development show that humankind can shift their darkest behaviors towards immense outcomes. Each time peacekeepers help mediate a tendency in a conflict or restore life in a community and another child is born in a peaceful world, their work is justified. In the end, their story illustrates that the world can become a better place – and they leave behind a legacy of victories over future conflicts and battles never fought.

Chapter 65: The Methods of Mediation

Discussing the idea of a peaceful world is impossible without asking how we handle our disagreements. Ever since humanity invented the first weapon, fighting back was our go-to solution to most problems. And although it's easy to say that we should just dismantle the guns, pack the tanks and send the boys home, it's equally important to consider what's going to replace all of that. Instead of war, what we need is mediation. Not the neighborhood warfare prevention program or critical event intervention, but actual mediators mediating, only on a planetary, global scale. We're talking about creating new institutions that can resolve those issues which caused wars. This would mean creating international peace organizations. Remember the UN? Imagine that, only much more hands-on and generally up close. Mediators would be locals, flown in, unable to leave until they come to some agreement. They would be the best in their field, capable of resolving any conflict, understanding the smallest of cultural nuances. They would be flown into the hotspots, invited all the feuding parties and then a separate party for some very tale talk. The negotiation, however, would be different from what you see in all those movies. Imagine not some Cold War, ice block of stranger in a suit arranging guard rows. Instead, think of some beautiful neutral space, a large vase full of your favorite flowers and a lot of common de Genève. And behind the mediator's desk, there wouldn't be a serious-looking bureaucrat; instead, imagine someone who deeply cares about you and understands you, the enemy, even better. That's not just mediation; that's advanced psychological techniques to choose a psychonegetic method. Just mediation is the beginning. The real drop-down comes after that. In addition to negotiating stuff not only with war avoidance but a lot about talking. First of all, they would work to figure out the top reason why conflicts arise in the first place. Economic injustice, history from insecurities, social issues. That's what they would be focusing on when creating the new world. Their aim would be fixing not only the consequences of the situation but also the causes, enabling communities to fix themselves. Or compliant. And there would be the important contribution of technology. Some fields such as wired bounds would be used to show enemies view each other's positions literally. Others such as minority groups such as social tools could be used to create and support peaceful mindsets. Finally, there is education. The entire world teaches the children his schoolroom mediation instead of math or science. They all grow up thinking about problems solved, understanding people also able to dusk and capable of taking the most active position. When they grow up, they use the discussions on a daily basis. Companies negotiate. Countries talk about the economic while its citizens talk about consuming upland. If a certain hatred grows spontaneously, however, they consult mediators. Such an approach can make a difference that tops the map. If humanity was able to make it job mediation, then they would have decided the space itself. This change in living encompasses the world, from global organizations to the school systems. This means replacing the out-group with victims or negotiation. It doesn't just mean avoiding war but expanding peace.

Chapter 66: Harmony as Heritage

These days our approach to conflict has grown way past the point where the simple need for warfare could ever justify it. We have turned our face to peace and not just as something to achieve but as a part of our identity. It is remarkable how international peace organizations have changed the way they operate by doing things that almost look like community building than they do conflict enduring. Just think about the possibility to stop responding with force but rather peacefully communicate with others to understand the root of the conflict that can be eliminated without violence. It is also interesting to see how operations work, like world therapists, helping people working out their issues on a global scale. What inspires the most is the way societies have also changed to teach the next generation more about handling disagreements. There are just more schools, public forums and other groups that are teaching negotiation and mediation. It almost looks like the whole peace initiative has become a heritage everybody wants to leave behind. I love thinking about this because it is not about preventing fights; it completely reshapes the way we think about disagreements completely. It is not anymore 'me versus they'; it is now 'we are fighting this together.' When it is a part of the culture, peace is not something to be achieved but to be cherished. And this trend gives hope. It shows that the violence and retaliation cycle is to be broken. People are ready to teach, learn and live in a way that has harmony as a basis of existence. And it is not just about acknowledging the transformation but the actual impact it has on life, governance and existence on this planet. It is creating the world where peace is a part of the heritage actively inheriting and cherishing.

Chapter 67: The Peaceful Everyday

Imagine waking up in a world where the morning news does not refer to conflicts and wars, but to achievements and collaborations. Yet, you will open your eyes in a peaceful community, where every day will be saturated with calm and there will be no conflicts and divisions, and nearly all relationships between people will be mediated by understanding and negotiations. Picture a lifestyle in which most aspects are based on communication and mutual respect. In the morning, before starting your day preparing for the job, you go to a gathering in your neighborhood, where everyone openly discusses the day's events and activities. People express their views without discrimination based on age, social class or occupation while still listening to one another in an effort to comprehend. The initial agenda is not only to address problems but also to help each other and the community together.

The role of education matters even more; it will no longer be focused only on the study of mathematics and physics but will also help people understand and develop pragmatic peacebuilding skills. Schools will provide a dialogue and empathy-based technique for solving disputes among children, averting outcomes with which we are now acquainted. The children will develop the belief that every voice has its own spirit, and that conflict is more harmful and less beneficial than collaboration. Such an approach will not be confined to schools; understanding of peace will be instilled in every aspect of a person's lifestyle from childhood and responsible behavior patterns will be assumed to remain a lifelong source of peace for humanity.

Likewise, such processes might be observed in the workforce. An office will transform into a common area where administrators work openly and transparently. Recreation and leisure are equally indicative of this culture of peace. People engage in sports and games for pleasure and camaraderie rather than to compete against one another or act aggressively. Art, from music to theater to the visual arts, frequently reflects the desire for connection and the sheer variety of human life.

Even the behavior of the cities and neighborhoods from which people hail exhibit this culture. Everything is constructed with the goal of facilitating interaction. Planes and architecture are designed as shared rather than singular areas. Gardens, parks and centers of community are the core of the world. People come together; the environment is a regular reminder of their tranquility. People will regularly have shared dinners at night. Neighbors nourish one other; tales are told and friendships are formed. Safety and security are in the air.

This sort of lifestyle is not merely about preventing calamity. It's about developing a culture of peace that pervades all you do. The way you behave at home. Everything you do for a living. How you act in a shared setting. This style of life may seem far-fetched, but it is not. It's merely a matter of assuming one's role more seriously. Everyone plays a role in keeping and promoting tranquility in all communities. A world created one day at a time.

Chapter 68: The Quiet Quotidian

In a world where the thunder of war is no longer heard, life begins to swing at a different pace. It is the trivial, unnoticeable things that are the main indicators of life in the world of peace. It is not the hum of the refrigerator but waking up to chat the chirping of birds and the neighbor. It is pleasant silence, the sense of well-being that many thousands of generations had dreamed of. Let's take a morning from daily life. People smile more often to each other and coffee is brewed and drunk not individually but together on porches. Commuting to work is no longer aggressive haste and a battle of horns but a joyful morning as employees gather in taxis. At work, it is no longer arrogant bosses and meetings behind closed doors. Discussions now resemble parliament and profit is not a bonus, but an integral part of the citizens and community. At lunchtime, everyone goes into the park, to his own garden or bank, grows vegetables and herbs and donates money to the library and school.

Education also differs and begins with kindness, camaraderie and non-conflict from kindergarten on. It is much easier to resolve controversy with words than with aggression. History and geography are taught not to blame someone for something but to enlighten the memory. In the end, each school garden becomes a model of the country, a relic.

In a peace-filled world, evenings are not spent locking doors behind oneself and checking the news to read the next story built on fear. In our world, communities are gathered around tables full of food, dancing to the tunes that musicians play to celebrate a meal. Libraries and community centers opened 24/7 play a vital role in this concept, continuously hosting workshops on anything from arts and crafts to meditation techniques. Public places are safe and illuminated, not because they are lit by streetlamps but because the community is willing to sacrifice its time to watch over its space.

Similarly, the concept of law enforcement changes. Community safety entails not law and order but de-escalation, support and solidarity amidst disagreement. Every single community peacekeeper is trained in psychological first aid and conflict resolution to bridge the outsider perspectives that maintain our life until it descends into chaos. It also changes the cessation of our day. Nighttime does not end with releasing one's breath and the press, replaced by a good night drive before bed. Every night community events flood the streets, resulting in open-air concerts where the song contains the identity of the people who sing them; this global tapestry of music woven into the fabric that makes up our world. Peace necessitates the existence of or an absence of challenge.

Chapter 69: Unity in Understanding

Think for a moment about a future where news of conflicts is supplanted by tales of collaboration and cooperation. In this envisioned world, societies are strong and tranquil, where laws aren't just for regulating disputes but are a way of life for every resident. The day might start with neighbors chatting in shared gardens instead of over divisive fences. From preschoolers to the elderly, everyone learns from one another, seizing opportunities for dialogue at nearly every encounter.

Schools prioritize teaching how to listen and communicate respectfully, embedding coexistence from the beginning. Work environments embrace constructive techniques; meetings focus on giving everyone a voice, transforming conflict from a disruption into an opportunity to explore new ideas and deepen understanding.

Community centers become vibrant hubs for discussions, helping those trying to see multiple perspectives but unsure how to proceed. Afternoons might be filled with workshops organized by the community, covering everything from art to science, each taught with an emphasis on contributing to societal cohesion.

Evenings bring people together for shared dinners in central courtyards where recipes and stories are exchanged, often concluding with music or dance that celebrates community bonds. Behind these daily interactions, there's a robust infrastructure supported by local governments that invest in initiatives fostering personal and shared growth. Policies ensure protection and equality, but it's the shared commitment to these principles that truly shapes daily life.

In this world, the principle of mutual understanding is not just an ideal but a tangible reality that governs everyday interactions. It's a testament to what can happen when a society is committed to unity and peace. This vision of daily life is not just a dream but a practical, collective endeavor, showing that peace and cooperation are not only possible but achievable with the right focus and commitment.

Chapter 70: Teach Peace Early

Teaching peace from an early age isn't just about sitting kids down and lecturing them on the horrors of war; it's about instilling values of empathy, understanding and cooperation from the start. Envision schools where conflict resolution and emotional intelligence are woven into the core curriculum, equipping the next generation with the tools needed not only to read and write but to interact harmoniously and with understanding in the world.

From an early age, we can influence attitudes before prejudices take hold. Imagine kindergartens where children learn the power of words, how to express feelings without causing harm and the importance of really listening to others. Such environments encourage collaboration over competition, teaching children that their voices matter, as do those of their peers.

As these children grow, their education evolves to include global cultures, religions and philosophies in an interactive setting. Instead of dry textbook learning, students would meet people from diverse backgrounds to hear their stories firsthand, dismantling the 'us versus them' mentality early on.

In high school, the educational approach could escalate to include courses on global issues that require students to propose collaborative solutions, possibly working with peers from other countries. This not only fosters cross-cultural bonds but also promotes a sense of global citizenship.

Technology could further enhance these lessons. Imagine virtual reality scenarios that let students experience life through another's eyes, or AI programs that facilitate real-time negotiation practice in safe, realistic settings.

By the time students mature into adults, they would be well-prepared not just academically but also emotionally and socially to lead a more peaceful future. They'd be equipped to challenge the status quo, understanding that differences do not equate to threats and that conflicts can be resolved with dialogue, not violence.

Such an education could be revolutionary, transforming schools into incubators for peace. This approach doesn't just aim to prevent conflicts; it cultivates a mindset where peace is the default and cooperation and respect are routine. This proactive cultivation of peace ensures we're not merely hoping for a better world; we're actively building it, one lesson at a time.

Chapter 71: Schools of Solidarity

Why shouldn't such values be embedded in the educational system from the very first stage? It's not only revolutionary but also crucial in shaping a future where harmony is valued over conflict. Imagine classrooms not just filled with lessons on math, history or biology, but also on how to coexist peacefully, satisfy mutual needs and cooperate regardless of differences in skin color or religious beliefs.

Starting with kindergartens, "Schools of Solidarity" can introduce children to empathy and understanding. Young minds are incredibly adaptable and can embrace critical life lessons, especially those that enhance their interpersonal skills. This early education isn't just about learning what the world is but how to positively shape it, beginning with their own communities.

As students progress, these foundational principles can evolve into more complex lessons on human relations and international politics. Middle schools could offer simulations where students engage in role-playing to resolve both real and fictional conflicts. By high school, the curriculum could look deeper into global histories, philosophies and movements advocating peace and social justice, supplemented by guest speakers like activists and diplomats involved in peacekeeping efforts.

A consistent element throughout all educational stages would be the integration of technology and social media to foster a global community. Students might engage in digital pen pal programs or collaborative international projects, allowing them to connect and share with peers worldwide without leaving their classrooms. This would not only enhance their global citizenship but also their understanding of diversity.

Assessment methods would also reflect this ethos of cooperation over competition. Instead of grading on a curve, evaluations could focus on group projects, community involvement and personal reflections, encouraging students to contemplate how they can contribute to societal peace.

By the time students graduate, they wouldn't just be prepared for the workforce or further education; they'd be equipped to be peacemakers in their personal lives, communities or on a global stage. This approach to education goes beyond academic achievement; it's about nurturing thoughtful, considerate citizens ready to live in and promote a peaceful society. This is not just about cultivating brilliant students but about fostering responsible, empathetic individuals who value peace as a fundamental part of life.

Chapter 72: Lessons in Love

Educating children from a young age in the principles of peace and cooperation is about creating lifelong habits of harmony and understanding, making these the essence of our education system. Imagine a schooling environment where children learn not only math and literacy but also how to resolve conflicts, appreciate diverse perspectives and genuinely care for one another.

Starting early with such education could profoundly transform our future. If children learn the art of negotiation, the value of active listening and the importance of settling disputes peacefully, these skills would become as natural to them as breathing. They would grow up in a world where collaboration is preferred over confrontation.

Imagine school projects designed to reinforce these principles. Children could engage in community service projects, learning firsthand how their efforts can positively impact their surroundings. Teachers could bring in stories from around the globe to celebrate diversity and teach the beauty of inclusiveness.

More than just preventing conflicts, this educational approach would cultivate a proactive spirit of peacemaking. Children could be tasked with creating 'peace projects' to propose ways to make their schools, communities or even the world, more peaceful places. These projects could range from writing letters to government officials advocating for peaceful policies to launching environmental initiatives.

Schools could also organize 'peace days,' where students from diverse backgrounds come together to share their cultures, traditions and dreams. These wouldn't just be educational sessions but celebrations of our shared human experience, emphasizing mutual respect and unity.

In this envisioned educational framework, every lesson is essentially a lesson in love; teaching children to love learning, to love each other and to love contributing to a peaceful world. The ripple effect of such education could be immense, creating a kinder, more cooperative global community.

This approach isn't just about shaping a child's academic path; it's about investing in their entire future and, by extension, the future of our society.

By prioritizing peace education, we are committing to a world where living in harmony is not just an ideal, but a practical, lived reality.

Chapter 73: A Century of Serenity

Imagine a world where the tumult of conflict has been relegated to the annals of history, and peace is not simply the interlude between wars but a state of permanence. We could live out what might be called a Century of Serenity. In this scenario, resources once squandered on defense are redirected to healthcare, education and sustainable practices that benefit the planet. Economies shift from arms races to focus on the well-being of citizens, with transformative results.

The pursuit of innovation and collaboration leads to breakthroughs in technology and medicine, making once incurable diseases preventable and healthcare universally accessible. This boosts global life expectancy and quality of life significantly. Education undergoes a transformation, moving away from nationalist ideologies to foster critical thinking and problem-solving skills. Schools worldwide enrich curriculums with global literature, arts and sciences, emphasizing the interconnectedness of our world.

Urban development mirrors this new focus on inclusivity and sustainability. Cities abound with green spaces, community gardens and efficient, non-polluting public transportation. Architecture not only serves functional purposes but also inspires, enhancing shared life and well-being.

Social interactions evolve in this era of peace; the notion of "the other" dissolves, replaced by curiosity and openness towards people from different backgrounds. The world feels smaller, more connected; a global festival where food, traditions and music are shared freely.

In this peaceful society, mental health becomes a priority, no longer neglected but cherished and supported by community infrastructure. People have more resources and time to invest in well-being, leading to resilient, compassionate societies.

The environmental impact is profound as well. With sustained peace, global efforts to combat climate change intensify. Renewable energy becomes the norm and conservation efforts are ingrained in daily life.

This vision isn't just a utopian dream; it's a plausible future if humanity chooses to prioritize peace. By valuing cooperation over conflict, empathy over enmity and community over chaos, we can create a world where everyone lives in harmony. Just imagining this possibility is life-affirming, isn't it?

Chapter 74: Cultures of Contentment

Consider a world where the echoes of conflict have dimmed into the background and societies prioritize satisfaction and well-being over competition and acquisition. This vision may seem idyllic, but envisioning daily life in a culture rooted in peace and joy offers intriguing possibilities.

In this peaceful scenario, people would wake up each morning without fear, freed from the pressures of climbing corporate ladders or outpacing their peers. Work would be more about purpose and contribution, aligning personal passions with the broader needs of the community to ensure everyone not only enjoys their work but also values their role within society.

Education would play a crucial role in fostering this culture of contentment. From an early age, children would learn about empathy, cooperation and the importance of mental and emotional health. Schools would go beyond mere fact delivery to teach children how to live well with others and contribute to healthy, supportive communities.

Healthcare would mirror this ethos of contentment, treating mental health with the same urgency and accessibility as physical health and emphasizing preventative care through holistic practices that balance the mind, body and spirit.

Economically, the focus would shift from relentless growth to sustainability and fairness. Success wouldn't be measured by GDP or market shares but by quality of life metrics such as happiness, community support and dignity in meeting basic needs. The economy would be restructured to ensure that everyone's needs are met and that no one is left behind in the pursuit of progress.

Urban planning would also transform, with a renewed focus on creating spaces that encourage connection, such as parks and community centers. Housing would be designed to foster a sense of belonging and community rather than isolation.

Leisure and entertainment would evolve to support this culture of contentment. The arts would flourish, with people engaging in activities that encourage bonding and connection with nature and each other, rather than promoting consumption and competition.

At the heart of this culture would be the relationships we cherish. With less stress and more support, people would invest more in their families, friendships and community ties, enriching their lives through shared experiences and mutual care.

By fostering an environment where contentment is the norm, not the exception, we could unlock tremendous potential for human creativity, cooperation and compassion. This vision of a content, peaceful society is not just a dream but a feasible pathway to a more prosperous, happy world.

Chapter 75: The Happiness Horizon

Let's look deeper into envisioning a future where peace is not just an aspiration but a foundational reality. Imagine waking up to a world where news broadcasts don't cover conflicts or wars but highlight remarkable achievements in global cooperation and community success stories. It's about transitioning from a mindset of survival and conflict to one of thriving and collaboration and seeing how such a change could profoundly enhance human happiness and development.

Imagine a society free from the stressors of geopolitical tensions or fears of violence. In this society, individuals could invest more energy in positive pursuits like innovation, creativity and personal growth. Educational systems would teach children to resolve differences through dialogue and empathy, rather than competition and dominance, nurturing a generation for whom peace is an integral part of life.

With peace as a cornerstone, we'd likely witness a surge in cultural exchanges and collaborations across previously rigid boundaries. Art, music, literature and technology would flourish as people share their creative expressions more freely, leading to unprecedented advancements that enrich our lives and broaden our perspectives.

Furthermore, the vast resources formerly allocated to military expenditures could be redirected towards healthcare, education and sustainability projects. This reallocation would enable us to tackle global challenges like climate change and health crises more effectively, without the distraction of competing for arms superiority.

This peaceful future would also redefine our concepts of success and prosperity. As global communities collaborate rather than compete, the pursuit of wealth could transform into a collective effort to enhance quality of life for all. Happiness and well-being would become the metrics by which we measure a country's success, superseding traditional indicators like GDP or military might.

We are exploring how embracing peace could fundamentally transform our global society, making it not only more harmonious but also fundamentally happier and more fulfilling. It's about envisioning a world where everyone works together to improve life and solve problems, not just for a privileged few but for everyone. This scenario isn't just a fantasy; it could become a reality if we commit to making peace a priority.

Part 6: A Brotherhood of Man

The final part of this book envisions a world where true equality is not just a concept but a reality. This final part explores a society where all barriers based on gender, sexual identity, race or economic status are dismantled, proposing a world where everyone has equal opportunities and rights and where individual worth is measured by humanity, not demographics or wealth.

Imagine a global family where differences are celebrated rather than used to divide. This section of the book delves into the realistic steps necessary to achieve such a society and examines the profound impacts these changes would have on everyone. It discusses creating an egalitarian world where every individual contributes to and benefits from a system that values each person equally.

While it may appear as a utopian dream, this part of the book lays out a detailed blueprint for building such a society. It covers necessary structural changes to eradicate systemic biases, explores innovative economic models that promote shared prosperity and discusses policy reforms that ensure equal rights and opportunities in practice, not just in theory.

Beyond structural and policy changes, this section emphasizes the cultural shifts needed to support and sustain equality. It addresses how we can foster a mindset that views diversity as a strength, educate our children to appreciate every person's unique contributions and create inclusive communities where everyone feels they belong.

The challenges and resistance to such transformative changes are also discussed, along with strategies to overcome them. The narrative draws inspiration from historical visionaries and current initiatives making strides toward more inclusive societies, offering lessons on how to effect change.

Ultimately, this part serves as a call to action, inviting each reader to play a role in shaping this new world. Whether through advocacy, education, policymaking or everyday interactions, everyone has a part in fostering a society that truly values every human being equally. It's a bold invitation to contribute to a legacy that will define the future; a world characterized not by division but by unity and mutual respect.

This journey toward a global brotherhood is envisioned not as mere fantasy but as an achievable reality if we commit to making it happen. It's about moving from imagination to action, from the current state to what could be and redefining humanity's narrative to one where equality, respect and brotherhood form the foundations of our daily lives. Join in this transformative venture, for a world where each individual's inherent worth is not only recognized but celebrated.

Chapter 76: Equality's Early Days

Here we tackle the shaky, sometimes stumbling steps we need to take as we begin to build a world where equality isn't just a lofty ideal but a lived reality. This journey is fascinating and admittedly a bit daunting, as it requires global societies to undergo monumental shifts.

The journey begins with sweeping changes in policies and a significant shift in public attitudes. While laws and regulations are the surface, the real challenge lies in changing hearts and minds. It's about ensuring that everyone not only has the same legal rights but actually feels they have equal opportunities to succeed and thrive.

Envision walking into a workplace where your background, education or connections don't define your value; instead, your ability to contribute and innovate does. In this environment, diversity is not just tolerated but celebrated as a crucial asset that enhances decision-making and creativity.

The media also plays a critical role. Early positive portrayals of this new egalitarian world can help dismantle long-held stereotypes and biases, planting seeds in the collective consciousness that grow into a new societal norm where equality feels as natural as breathing.

However, the path isn't smooth. Setbacks occur; moments when old prejudices resurface and fear and misunderstanding threaten to derail progress. These are the times when communities need to unite, engage in difficult conversations and address the issues holding them back.

In the early stages, symbols of past inequality; such as statues and building names; are often reassessed. What do these symbols represent in our new era? Debates may rage, but over time, more inclusive symbols emerge, reflecting the values of a society striving for equality.

Local actions, like public forums and educational programs, become crucial as people begin to understand and embrace their roles in this transformation. It's not just about changing laws but about changing how we view each other and ourselves.

The beauty of this early phase lies in its raw, earnest striving towards something fundamentally right. Despite the missteps, each one teaches us something vital, helping to solidify the foundations of a truly egalitarian society.

As we envision those early days, we see a mix of chaos and hope, challenges and victories. It's a reminder that while the road to equality may be long and winding, it's paved with the potential for profound human connection and a shared future that values every person equally. This isn't just a dream; it's a possible reality that begins with bold, determined steps forward.

Chapter 77: The Struggle and the Success

Envisioning a truly egalitarian world involves reflecting on the path from our current reality to a more ideal future. This transition isn't instantaneous; it's a series of efforts, challenges and significant achievements. The journey is marked by both trials and triumphs. Initially, resistance might seem formidable, emerging from entrenched social norms, economic systems that favor a few and deep-seated prejudices that many are not even aware of. This resistance is active, opposing the necessary changes to create balance.

Yet, the narrative of struggle is complemented by a stronger push towards fairness. It's inspiring to see diverse individuals from various backgrounds unite with a common goal of equality. These champions of change drive community initiatives, advocate for policy reforms and promote a society where equality isn't just an ideal but a reality.

As we navigate these challenges, successes begin to surface. Imagine communities where marginalized voices now lead discussions about their future. Picture schools where all children receive equal education and opportunities, irrespective of their background. Envision workplaces where advancement is based on merit alone, disregarding differences.

These aren't just hypothetical scenarios; they are tangible outcomes of persistent efforts by dedicated individuals and groups. Each victory, no matter how small, creates a ripple effect, encouraging more people to advocate for equality and make their own impact.

This journey is a collective endeavor, where every small step forward is celebrated as a societal win. The camaraderie developed among those fighting for equality exemplifies the type of society we aim to create; one where everyone supports one another. The triumphs that emerge from these struggles are sweet not only because of the victories themselves but also for what they represent; a movement towards a world that lives up to our ideals of humanity.

Though the road to equality can be daunting, the vision of a global brotherhood where every individual is valued equally propels us forward, inspiring us to tackle the challenges and embrace the successes that lie ahead. This is more than a dream; it's a viable reality that starts with determined, collective steps towards a fairer world.

Chapter 78: Every Person's Place

In envisioning a truly egalitarian world, where every individual finds their place, we think about achieving a societal model where everyone is valued equally. Imagine a day when our considerations aren't about who has more or where someone is from, but seeing each other simply as fellow travelers on the journey of life. This dream involves moving beyond the deep-seated biases and disparities that have long divided us.

Imagine living in neighborhoods where diversity is not just tolerated but celebrated, where every child goes to school knowing they have as much a chance at success as their peers, no matter their background. Envision workplaces where opportunities are based solely on one's passion and skills, not their gender, age or ethnicity, where promotions are merit-based and pay disparities are a thing of the past.

In this world, economic systems would be redesigned to ensure that basic needs like food, shelter and healthcare are met for everyone, promoting economies that thrive for all, not just a select few. Such changes would not be about charity but about justice and fairness.

Visualize a society where law enforcement and justice systems operate with complete integrity and fairness, where trust between communities and those sworn to protect them is the norm. Imagine redefined social structures where social mobility is genuinely achievable and the barriers that have historically marginalized some are dismantled.

In such a society, public gatherings; from festivals to park outings; would reflect this new ethos, with communities vibrant with the energy of understanding and respecting diversity. Art and culture would thrive, telling the stories of all people and celebrating the mosaic of human life.

This vision requires hard, practical work. It involves crafting policies with empathy, designing educational systems that teach respect and understanding from early ages and ensuring that every voice, no matter how historically silenced, is heard and valued in shaping our common future.

It's not just a hopeful thought but a firm belief that we can achieve this world, step by step. We begin in our communities, through our conversations and with our actions. Each one of us holds a piece of this vast puzzle and by assembling these pieces together, the image of a truly egalitarian society; where each person's value is acknowledged and celebrated; becomes clearer. This is the world we aim to create, where equality permeates all aspects of life and our collective efforts foster a global brotherhood that values every individual equally.

Chapter 79: The End of Exclusion

Creating a world without exclusion is akin to opening a door where everyone is genuinely welcome, regardless of their origins or appearance. This involves dismantling all societal barriers related to gender, race, economic status etc., and building an inclusive community in their place. It's about more than just removing barriers; it's about constructing a new reality centered on inclusivity.

To fully appreciate the end of exclusion, consider all aspects of daily life and the systemic structures we engage with; from employment and education to healthcare and the judicial system. Education needs to evolve beyond basic subjects to teach children the importance of embracing and celebrating diversity. This curriculum fosters understanding and appreciation for different cultures and experiences from an early age.

In the workplace, ending exclusion extends beyond equal opportunity employment; it's about creating environments where every individual's voice is heard and valued. This includes establishing mentorship programs that extend beyond traditional candidates and promoting leadership that mirrors the workforce's diversity, recognizing that varied perspectives drive innovation and progress.

In healthcare, ending exclusion involves dismantling biases that affect treatment accessibility and the quality of care received by different demographic groups. This means conducting research that addresses the diverse medical needs and responses of various populations.

The justice system also requires significant reform to ensure laws and law enforcement practices do not disproportionately affect certain groups. This means guaranteeing that justice is not only a concept but a reality reflected in every legal proceeding and outcome.

On a personal level, ending exclusion transforms everyday interactions with neighbors, colleagues and even strangers, encouraging us to see each other as fellow humans with unique dreams, challenges and rights, rather than as 'others.' It means fostering open, enriching conversations that were once avoided or uncomfortable.

Achieving this isn't just a utopian ideal but a practical endeavor requiring policy changes, community initiatives and individual commitments to inclusivity. It calls for participation from everyone, from policymakers and grassroots activists to ordinary individuals who choose to make inclusion a personal mission.

The elimination of exclusion marks the beginning of a truly connected world where societal divisions dissolve into unity, where everyone has an equal chance at success and happiness, enhanced by their identities. As we work towards this goal, we start to see the seeds of change blossom into a garden of diversity that is celebrated, not just tolerated. This transformation is not just a dream but a potential reality that begins with decisive, collective actions toward a more inclusive society.

Chapter 80: Rights and Respect

Creating a world where every person is treated with equal respect involves a significant recalibration of our societal norms concerning rights and dignity. It's not merely about implementing new policies but about fundamentally reweaving the fabric of society so that respect for every individual, irrespective of their background, is inherent and unquestioned.

Envision a society where each person you encounter greets you with a nod, acknowledging your inherent worth; where respect is as commonplace as a simple "hello." This mutual respect compels us to treat each other better, influencing our laws, educational systems and business practices.

Bringing this vision to life means that rights must transcend being mere legal formalities to become tangible experiences. In workplaces, this goes beyond having equal employment laws on the books to creating environments where all employees, regardless of their demographics, feel genuinely welcomed and valued. It's about fostering a culture where mentorship and opportunities for advancement are accessible to everyone, based on merit and contribution rather than background.

In educational settings, promoting respect and equality extends beyond the curriculum. It involves teachers actively modeling respect for each student's ideas and encouraging an environment where every child believes they can achieve greatness, without barriers or biases.

Wider community engagement is also crucial. Respectful urban planning would ensure that parks, libraries and public spaces are welcoming to all, not just those from affluent areas. Public services should cater to the diverse needs of the community, ensuring accessibility and inclusivity.

The role of the media is pivotal in shaping perceptions and breaking down stereotypes. By promoting narratives that highlight shared human experiences and dreams rather than differences, media can play a significant role in fostering a more inclusive society.

Moreover, respecting rights requires active participation from everyone. It involves creating platforms where diverse voices can be heard and valued, contributing to a richer dialogue that influences public policy and community initiatives.

On a global scale, international relations should be based on mutual respect, viewing each country as an equal partner, regardless of economic or military strength.

A society deeply rooted in rights and respect is not just a lofty ideal; it's a practical and achievable goal that promises a healthier, more stable and prosperous future for everyone. By ensuring that everyone's rights are not only recognized but also cherished, we pave the way for a society that thrives on the collective potential of all its members.

Chapter 81: Celebrating Diversity

Celebrating diversity envisions a world where everyone brings something unique to the table, enhancing a vibrant and dynamic society. It's a world where differences are not merely tolerated but truly celebrated, forming a beautiful mosaic of human experiences.

Imagine a daily life where recognizing and valuing each individual's unique identity is commonplace. This involves listening to various voices and stories, each enriching the broader human narrative. Every community event, festival and classroom lesson becomes an opportunity to explore and appreciate the rich tapestry of human life.

Visualize walking through a neighborhood vibrant with diverse cultural celebrations, where multiple languages meld with music from across the globe. Food from every continent is a street corner away and neighbors share not just meals but their lives. Children grow up valuing every skin color, appreciating every accent and learning from stories that span the globe.

In the workplace, celebrating diversity means creating environments where everyone, regardless of their background, can thrive. It's about more than equal opportunity; it's about fostering a culture where diverse thoughts and ideas fuel innovation and growth. Every team member is encouraged to bring their whole selves to work, knowing their unique perspectives are essential for success.

Education plays a crucial role in this celebration. Schools become hubs of cultural exchange, where the curriculum includes global histories and realities and teachers facilitate discussions on personal uniqueness with empathy and understanding.

Legal and social systems must evolve to ensure everyone is treated equally under the law, with proactive measures to address historical injustices. This includes reforming the criminal justice system and creating economic policies that promote fairness.

Celebrating diversity also happens in everyday interactions; smiling at a neighbor, inquiring about their heritage with genuine interest and listening; truly listening; to their responses. It's about standing against discrimination, not only when it affects you but especially when it does not.

This vision of diversity is not just an ideal but involves practical steps toward a more inclusive society. It's about each of us playing a role, from policy changes and community programs to personal commitments to inclusivity. As we strive toward this goal, we create not just a more equitable world but a whole world where everyone's place is acknowledged and celebrated.

Chapter 82: Artistic Expressions of Unity

Envisioning a world where everyone is interconnected, we see a vibrant tapestry formed not just from our similarities but our diverse backgrounds. The arts play a pivotal role in this vision, acting as a reflection of our societies and the personal journeys of the artists. In this imagined world, every artwork, song and performance contributes to a narrative of unity and shared human experience, making the arts a powerful expression of our collective aspiration towards unity.

This diversity of expression is what makes the vision so beautiful. Artists from every corner of the globe bring their unique perspectives, blending traditional and contemporary influences to create art that resonates universally. Imagine a mural in a bustling city square, collaboratively painted by artists from various nations, each illustrating their cultural interpretation of unity. Or a concert where musicians from different ethnic backgrounds merge their traditional sounds into a harmonious symphony that transcends language and culture.

Art festivals and exhibitions in this world transcend mere artistic showcases; they become dynamic platforms for dialogue and mutual understanding. Picture a film festival focusing on reconciliation and cooperation, where filmmakers from regions once marked by conflict come together to co-create films that not only address past grievances but also envision a shared future.

The influence of such artistic collaborations extends beyond the arts community, impacting fashion, design and other creative industries. Fashion weeks might feature collections that blend styles and materials from across the globe, challenging traditional beauty norms and promoting a broader, inclusive aesthetic.

Moreover, the impact of a globally united artistic community would significantly alter educational curricula. Schools around the world would teach art not only as a technical skill but as an essential medium for cultural exchange and mutual respect. From a young age, children would learn that creativity knows no borders and that through art, they can connect with and understand their global peers.

The ripple effects of these artistic expressions are profound. They help dismantle the invisible barriers that have long divided us, fostering a deeper understanding across different cultures and communities. By celebrating our differences and discovering our shared humanity through art, we pave the way toward a future where the concept of a global brotherhood is not just an ideal but a tangible reality. In this world, every human being is valued and every voice finds expression in a grand mosaic of creativity that celebrates our collective journey toward unity.

Chapter 83: The Sciences of Sympathy

Exploring how empathy can revolutionize the scientific field leads to the exploration of sympathy. This approach views science not just as a tool for technological advancement and industrial progress but as a critical component in fostering human connections and building a more empathetic and unified society.

Imagine scientists, researchers and technologists worldwide focusing on projects that extend beyond mere profit and innovation. Consider endeavors aimed at developing sustainable technologies to combat climate change or medical advancements that are accessible to all, regardless of geographical or economic status.

Education plays a crucial role in this paradigm. It's about teaching young scientists not only the facts but also the social implications of their work. How does a new invention impact communities? Can it improve lives? Does it bring people together or drive them apart? These questions would be central to a revamped curriculum that emphasizes the impact of scientific endeavors on human relationships and the environment.

Moreover, the power of collaboration in this context is transformative. By fostering international partnerships that cross borders, cultures and disciplines, the scientific community can model global unity. These collaborations help dismantle prejudices and foster a mutual understanding that goes beyond traditional barriers, creating a collective vision for the future.

The role of empathy in science can serve as a catalyst for profound change. It's about enhancing life quality for everyone, healing our planet and bridging divides between diverse groups. The potential ripple effects of such a science approach could lead to a world where technological and humanitarian advancements are intertwined, promoting a more equitable society.

This redefined approach also alters the definition of success for scientists. Being a top researcher or working in a renowned lab is complemented by the impact one's work has on improving lives and uplifting communities. Success in this context comes from contributing to a world where every individual can benefit from scientific progress.

This could lay the foundation for a new era where technology and compassion are seamlessly integrated, leading us not only to a smarter but also a kinder world. This is a vision of a future where our scientific pursuits help us better understand not only the world around us but also each other, striving towards a more connected and empathetic global community.

Chapter 84: A World Woven Together

In envisioning how a globally connected society might influence our arts, culture and sciences, we imagine a world where every creative expression; from urban murals to poignant films; reflects a diverse spectrum of human experiences. This interconnectedness not only enriches each artistic and scientific endeavor but also helps to forge a deeper human connection across various cultures.

Consider music festivals where African rhythms, Western harmonies and Eastern melodies blend, symbolizing our shared human experience through the universal language of music. Art galleries would juxtapose indigenous artworks with avant-garde European sculptures, each piece contributing to a larger narrative of global unity and understanding.

In science, this global integration transforms research paradigms, with collaborative projects across borders tackling universal challenges like climate change and health disparities. Such cooperation could lead to breakthroughs previously unimaginable in isolated research environments.

Education systems worldwide would adapt, teaching not just academic subjects but also the value of cultural diversity and global cooperation. Students would learn to appreciate their impact on the world, thinking globally while acting locally.

Technological advancements would support this vision, with innovations like real-time translation devices and social platforms designed to foster understanding and dismantle divisions.

This scenario is not just a utopian dream but a plausible future where the barriers that once divided us are overcome, leading to a world where every individual contribution is valued equally. The beauty of this vision lies in its promise of harmonious coexistence and the enriched lives resulting from our shared interdependence. It's an inspiring testament to how our interconnectedness can profoundly enhance our lives.

Chapter 85: Democratic Dreams

Imagine a world where democracy transcends its traditional boundaries and becomes a collective dream that we all actively shape. This vision involves everyone having a voice, not just those with influence or financial power. It's about transforming governance into a truly collaborative process where decision-making is shared and deeply democratic.

This concept of democracy goes beyond merely voting in elections every few years. It involves ongoing, real-time input into the decisions that affect our daily lives. Technology could play a crucial role here, facilitating instant feedback loops and participatory platforms where our input is not just heard but also acted upon.

We'd also need to rethink representation. Imagine if our leaders truly reflected the community's diversity; not just as political figureheads but as facilitators who amplify the voices of all, especially those historically marginalized. This democratic reform would ensure that decision-making bodies mirror the actual demographics of the population, encompassing all.

Moreover, transparency would be paramount. No more backroom deals or mysterious policy decisions. Instead, everything would be open, with clear, understandable information accessible to everyone. This level of transparency would foster trust and accountability, enabling meaningful participation in governance.

Education would play a vital role in this democratic vision. We'd need to ensure that from a young age, people understand not just the mechanics of government but also the importance of their engagement. Education would focus on critical thinking over rote learning, teaching individuals how to question, critique and constructively engage in public discourse.

Economic policies would also align with democratic values, ensuring no disproportionate influence from the wealthy. Measures might include innovative approaches like universal basic income or new forms of public ownership that ensure everyone has a stake and a say in economic development.

In this envisioned world, democracy is not just a political structure but a way of life, shaping every interaction and decision to ensure that everyone's voice contributes to the collective well-being. This kind of democracy might seem like a dream, but it's a dream worth striving for; a fairer, more inclusive world where everyone has the opportunity to thrive. This is the essence of the democratic dream; a governance model that truly reflects the will and welfare of all its people.

Chapter 86: Participatory Politics

Imagine a world where politics is not just a duty but an integral part of daily life, where every voice is not only spoken but truly heard. Here, participatory politics isn't just an achievement but the very essence of society. What if every government decision was influenced by your input, where no policy was enacted without collective input? This radical approach extends democracy to its deepest roots, ensuring no one feels left out.

In this envisioned society, technology enhances participation, making it easier for everyone to engage in governance. Picture a digital platform where you can log in, discuss and vote on policies affecting your community and beyond. Local meetings would no longer be sparsely attended events but vibrant, accessible discussions held at various times and available via live streams, making engagement practical and enjoyable.

Transparency in this world isn't just an ideal; it's the standard. No more decisions made behind closed doors or entangled in legalese; every process is open for scrutiny and the rationale behind decisions is clear to all. This ensures that governance is something you can trust and actively participate in, because it's transparent and inclusive.

Moreover, imagine a society where even those traditionally marginalized have direct channels to influence policy. Efforts would be made to ensure all groups, regardless of socio-economic status, have access to these participatory platforms. Mobile units or community volunteers could assist those less tech-savvy or living in remote areas.

The outcome? Policies that are more inclusive and comprehensive because they're shaped by the people they affect. This leads to a government that genuinely reflects the will and needs of its populace. While managing everyone's input and ensuring equal voice can be challenging, it's a significant step toward a more equitable society.

Participatory politics transforms governance from a concept of power to one of empowerment. It reimagines politics, turning passive citizens into active participants in shaping their future. This approach isn't just about making better decisions; it's about making those decisions together. By actively building a world of equality, we do more than dream of a fair society; we create it.

Chapter 87: Voices Valued

Envision a society that is truly egalitarian, where not just every voice counts but one that is actively listened to. We're talking about governance that is not only for the people but also by the people. Imagine a world where democracy isn't just a system but a way of life, where collaborative decision-making extends beyond the ballot box and into every facet of daily living.

Picture a world where everyone has a say in decisions that impact their lives, from community issues like education and neighborhood developments to major national policies on economics and the environment. It's about enhancing the principle of "one person, one vote" to ensure that everyone's experiences and viewpoints are genuinely recognized and valued.

Reflecting on how technology could support this new form of governance, consider tools that provide real-time feedback and secure, transparent platforms for public input. Governance becomes a more transparent, engaging and active process. It's more than sporadic town hall sessions or periodic elections; it's a continuous dialogue with citizens.

Imagine starting your day with notifications on your device asking for your input on a new community recycling initiative, followed by a live-streamed council session on public transportation reforms, where your comments could directly influence the final decisions. Such interactions would foster a sense of ownership and responsibility among community members, encouraging them to actively participate in shaping the society they live in.

This approach also challenges traditional power hierarchies. By valuing every voice equally, we can overcome persistent prejudices and biases that often silence minority groups. It's about recognizing that wisdom and valuable insights can come from anyone, regardless of their status or background.

Moreover, we must address potential challenges and criticisms of such a system, such as the risk of decision fatigue from constant polling, and ensuring inclusivity despite the digital divide. These are real issues that require balanced solutions, possibly involving a mix of digital and in-person engagements to ensure that everyone can participate.

Ultimately, we aim to depict a society where governance is intrinsically linked to community spirit and policymaking involves as much listening as it does leading. In this envisioned world, the value of a voice isn't determined by its loudness but by the authenticity and sincerity behind it. It's a world where every opinion is not only heard but also integral to the societal fabric, fostering a robust, dynamic and inclusive future.

Chapter 88: The Global Family

As I thought on writing about what a global family might entail, I reflected on the diverse families I've known; each unique in size, dynamics and complexity. This led me to wonder, what if we extended the best aspects of these familial connections worldwide? Let's explore the idea of expanding our sense of kinship to encompass not only every human being but also all forms of life and our shared environment.

Imagine stepping outside and seeing not just a tree, but recognizing it as a living entity with which we share an intrinsic connection. This perspective isn't about literal tree-hugging (though that's fine if it's your thing!) but rather about appreciating the roles each component plays within our ecological web. It's about realizing that the well-being of our planet directly influences our health and the prospects for future generations.

The foundation of envisioning a global family starts with empathy and education. From a young age, children would learn about both human history and the history of the natural world, emphasizing the crucial impact our environment has on our survival and quality of life. This education wouldn't stop after childhood but would be a lifelong pursuit, fostering a profound respect for nature and an understanding of how deeply interconnected our lives are with the ecosystems around us.

This perspective then expands to include all of humanity. Each individual, no matter where they are in the world, would be considered a sibling. This requires rethinking our social structures to ensure that everyone has access to essential resources like food, water, shelter and education; rights that are currently distributed unevenly across the globe. Addressing these disparities head-on is crucial for the realization of a true global family.

Technology could significantly accelerate this vision. With the power of the internet and digital communication, we've already seen barriers between people begin to crumble. There's potential to use these tools not just for economic growth or social networking, but to foster a sense of global unity and responsibility. Imagine platforms designed not just for sharing updates but for exchanging resources, educational tools and direct support to those in need.

Governance would also need restructuring to truly reflect a system that is by the people, for all people. This means decision-making processes would need to consider the well-being of every global family member, not just a select few. This could entail a significant shift in how we view politics and leadership, focusing on collective global well-being rather than narrow national interests.

What ultimately binds this global family together is a shared commitment to each other and our planet. Acts of kindness and cooperation would become the norm. Businesses would aim not just for profit but for positive impacts on communities and the environment. Urban planning would prioritize sustainability and green spaces.

I encourage you to think about the role you might play in this global family. Whether it's educating others, volunteering your time or working on projects that bridge divides, every effort counts in building a family; especially one as large as ours. By fostering true global kinship, we're talking about a revolution in how we connect with the world and each other. It's ambitious, but it's not just a dream. Like any family, it requires work, patience, understanding and most importantly, love. Here's to dreaming big and building a family that spans the entire globe.

Chapter 89: Stewardship of the Sphere

As we near the conclusion of our journey in this book, I'd like to focus on something crucial; not just how we treat one another but how we treat our home, Earth. Let's look into reimagining our relationship with the planet. This chapter is not merely an environmental plea; it's integral to our vision for a global brotherhood.

We've discussed breaking down societal barriers and fostering equality among humans. Yet, there's a significant interconnected component we cannot overlook: our ecological responsibilities. What's the value of social harmony if it exists on a planet that struggles to support life?

Stewardship here is viewed not just as a duty but as a privilege and joy. It's about embracing the role of custodians of Earth, ensuring our actions consider their environmental impact. This form of stewardship aligns closely with our broader goals of equality and peace; recognizing that a planet in crisis impacts everyone, indiscriminately.

True stewardship involves more than adhering to a "do no harm" philosophy; it's about proactive improvement and nurturing of our environment. Sustainable practices become the norm globally, from urban planning that incorporates green, breathable buildings that contribute to local biodiversity, to agricultural methods that sustain soil health and judicious water use.

We also tackle equity in environmental responsibility. Historically, the burden of environmental degradation hasn't been evenly distributed. Wealthier nations often shield themselves from the worst effects, leaving poorer, less resilient areas to suffer. Correcting these imbalances is crucial, ensuring that environmental resilience resources and technologies are accessible across borders and barriers.

Moreover, this stewardship extends beyond human-centric concerns, advocating for policies and practices that respect all life forms. This holistic approach ensures that our fellow Earth inhabitants, from the smallest insects to the largest mammals, have their rights to exist and thrive protected.

Contemplate what it means to leave a legacy of stewardship. It's about instilling a sense of ecological ethics in future generations, inspired by hope for a richer, more vibrant world, not fear of disaster. Our environmental actions are framed as contributions to a legacy that celebrates life in all its forms.

Remember that stewardship of the sphere isn't just a chapter in a book; it's a chapter in our lives, integral to building a truly egalitarian society. Let's not forget that peace with our planet is as crucial as peace among people. It's all connected, all essential. Let's embrace the grand responsibility and adventure of being the stewards our future needs.

Chapter 90: The Legacy of Love

As we conclude our exploration, it's essential to reflect on the kind of legacy we aspire to leave behind; a legacy that embodies the principles of a truly egalitarian world. This final chapter isn't just about summarizing our hopes and dreams; it's about solidifying them into something enduring, something that will not only survive us but also flourish long after we are gone.

Consider the significance of constructing a legacy founded on love. This goes beyond mere sentimentality or episodic acts of charity; it's about establishing systems, communities and global connections rooted in empathy, equity and environmental stewardship. Love here is not transient but a cornerstone of civilization.

Imagine a future where our global kinship extends to all life forms, beginning with a fundamental shift in perspective. Every policy, community action and global initiative could start by asking, "Does this serve all life with love?" This simple question could dramatically alter our actions and decisions, influencing everything from local community activities to significant global policies.

Building Sustainable Communities: The journey begins at home, both literally and metaphorically. Creating communities that reflect our love for life involves more than just sustainable habits like recycling or biking. It includes designing living spaces and infrastructures that respect and nurture the environment and all its inhabitants. Envision cities with green roofs, energy systems that regenerate rather than deplete and urban plans that integrate nature into our daily spaces.

Economics of Empathy: Our economic systems need transformation to shift from exploitation to sustainability. An empathetic economy would assess resources not by their market value but by their ability to sustain life. It would reward businesses not just for their profitability but for their impact on the environment and all affected life forms. In this economy, success is measured by the well-being distributed, not the wealth accumulated.

Education for Empathy: Education should teach us not only how to survive but how to coexist. From an early age, children should learn empathy, cooperation and ecological stewardship. Schools would become gardens of diversity, nurturing each student's unique contributions to our collective well-being, moving away from competitive learning towards a shared exploration of life's complexities.

Global Governance for the Greater Good: At a global level, governance should act more as caretakers than rulers. Decisions should be made transparently and inclusively, using technology to facilitate widespread participation in the democratic process, ensuring every voice contributes to our shared decision-making.

The True Test of Our Legacy: The durability of this legacy will be tested by its resilience; how well it handles the challenges and changes our planet faces. This isn't about crafting a conflict-free utopia but about forging a society capable of addressing challenges through cooperation, respect and foresight.

As we close this book, consider your role in this legacy. Each of us influences our environment through daily acts of kindness, the choices we make as consumers, citizens and community members. Imagine a world where each commitment to this path collectively weaves a global tapestry of sustainability and respect.

This shared dream, this future we build, this enduring legacy we aspire to; let's move forward together, guided by love, to make this vision a reality.

Epilogue

As we conclude this journey, I find myself filled with hope and a touch of anticipation. I dream of a future where the concepts we've explored throughout this book aren't just theoretical possibilities but tangible realities. Imagine a world where we live in harmony, no longer divided by the barriers that have long dictated our interactions with each other and our planet.

John Lennon might have been one of the first to invite us to imagine such a world, but he certainly wasn't the last. Every day, more and more of us dream of peace, unity and shared existence. I hope that as you turn the pages of this book and return to your daily life, you carry a piece of this dream with you.

Perhaps you will join us in this quest. And maybe, just maybe, someday we will see the world live as one. Here's to that day; may it come sooner than we think.

As I pen these final words, the vision of such a world seems almost within our grasp, like a delicate bubble floating just ahead, shimmering with the colors of possibility. This vision isn't born from naivety but as a deliberate beacon guiding us through the fog of discord and division. It's a call to action, an invitation for each reader to become an architect of this new world. Through our choices, actions and voices, we have the power to shape society.

Imagine a future where generations look back at this pivotal moment in history and recognize our courage to dream. Let this book be more than a collection of ideas; let it be a spark that ignites further inspiration, spreading light where there was once division.

As you resume your daily routines, remember that each moment offers a choice and every interaction is an opportunity to foster understanding rather than conflict. What if each of us embraced this role as ambassadors of unity and peace? What might our world then look like?

I leave these thoughts not as a conclusion but as a beginning of a dialogue to be continued in your lives and communities. The dream of a unified world, of enduring peace and mutual respect, is an ongoing journey; one that extends beyond the pages of this book into each of our lives.

So, echoing John Lennon's words, I hope you'll join us. Together, there is no limit to what we can achieve. The world can indeed live as one; a symphony of diverse voices, each contributing their unique note, yet together creating a harmony that resonates through the ages.

Here's to us, to our shared journey and to the day when our dreams are reflected in the reality of a world united in peace and love. May we all help bring about that day.

www.ingramcontent.com/pod-product-compliance
Lightning Source LLC
Chambersburg PA
CBHW030307160726
47992CB00005B/1913